TASMANIA

TRAVEL GUIDE

2024 EDITION

TABLE OF CONTENTS

INTRODUCTION

GETTING THERE

HOBART

INTRODUCTION

Welcome to Tasmania

Welcome to Tasmania, a captivating island state nestled in the southern part of Australia. Renowned for its breathtaking landscapes, rich cultural heritage, and unique wildlife, Tasmania has earned its reputation as a must-visit destination for travelers seeking a one-of-a-kind experience.

Tasmania, often referred to as the "Apple Isle," is the 26th-largest island in the world. Separated from the Australian mainland by the Bass Strait, it is surrounded by the Southern Ocean to the south and the Tasman Sea to the east. The state comprises the main island of Tasmania and numerous smaller islands, each contributing to the region's diverse geography.

One of Tasmania's most striking features is its pristine wilderness. Home to World Heritage-listed national parks and reserves, the island boasts a remarkable array of natural wonders. From the iconic Cradle Mountain to the untouched beauty of Southwest National Park, Tasmania's landscapes are a paradise for nature enthusiasts. The vibrant colors of the Bay of Fires, the ancient beauty of the Tarkine rainforest, and the rugged splendor of the Freycinet Peninsula offer a tapestry of experiences for every traveler.

Tasmania's isolation has led to the evolution of a unique ecosystem. The state is a haven for wildlife, including iconic species like the Tasmanian devil, the pademelon, and the elusive Tasmanian tiger. With a wealth of bird species and marine life, the island provides ample opportunities for wildlife enthusiasts and birdwatchers to indulge in their passion.

Beyond its natural wonders, Tasmania is steeped in a rich cultural heritage. The Tasmanian Aboriginal people, with a history dating back thousands of years, have left a significant mark on the island's identity. Visitors can explore ancient rock art sites, learn about Dreamtime stories, and gain insights into the enduring connection between the Aboriginal community and their ancestral lands.

Tasmania's charm extends to its quaint towns and vibrant cities. Hobart, the capital, is a captivating blend of history and modernity. Its iconic waterfront, bustling Salamanca Market, and the historic Battery Point district are just a few highlights. Launceston, in the north, offers a laid-back atmosphere and is a gateway to the Tamar Valley wine region. Meanwhile, the coastal town of Devonport welcomes visitors with its maritime history and the spirit of the Bass Strait.

For those seeking adventure, Tasmania is a playground of possibilities. Hiking enthusiasts can tackle the renowned Overland Track, a trek through some of the world's most pristine wilderness. Water lovers can explore the coastline by kayak or embark on a thrilling white-water rafting expedition. The state's diverse terrain ensures that outdoor enthusiasts of all levels can find an activity that suits their interests.

Tasmania's culinary scene is a testament to the island's fertile lands and pristine waters. With an abundance of fresh produce, the state has gained acclaim for its food and wine. From the succulent Tasmanian salmon to the crisp sweetness of local apples, every bite is a celebration of the island's natural bounty. Indulge in farm-to-table dining experiences, explore local markets, and savor the flavors that define Tasmania's gastronomic identity.

Understanding Tasmania's climate is key to planning a memorable visit. The island experiences four distinct seasons, each offering a unique perspective of its beauty. Spring brings blossoming flowers and milder temperatures, while summer invites outdoor adventures under the clear skies. Autumn paints the landscapes with warm hues, and winter transforms the mountainous regions into a snow-covered wonderland. Regardless of the season, Tasmania's allure remains constant.

In essence, Tasmania welcomes you with open arms to a world of natural wonders, cultural richness, and unparalleled adventures. Whether you seek the tranquility of a secluded beach, the thrill of an outdoor expedition, or the warmth of a historic town, Tasmania promises an experience that will linger in your memories. As you embark on your journey through this island paradise, allow Tasmania to captivate your senses and reveal the beauty that defines this extraordinary corner of the world.

Best Time to Visit

Tasmania experiences four distinct seasons: summer, autumn, winter, and spring. Each season showcases the island's natural beauty in different ways, catering to a range of interests from outdoor adventures to cultural explorations.

Summer (December to February):

Summer is the peak tourist season in Tasmania, and for good reason. The island comes alive with vibrant colors as flowers bloom, and the landscapes are bathed in warm sunlight. The temperatures range from mild to warm, making it an ideal time for outdoor activities such as hiking, camping, and wildlife spotting.

The coastal areas, including popular destinations like Freycinet Peninsula, become particularly inviting during summer. The crystal-clear waters are perfect for swimming, kayaking, and other water-based activities. Festivals and events also dot the summer calendar, offering a chance to immerse yourself in Tasmania's unique culture.

Autumn (March to May):

Autumn ushers in a spectacular display of foliage as the leaves transform into a tapestry of reds, oranges, and yellows. The weather remains relatively mild, making it an excellent time to explore Tasmania's national parks and hiking trails. The famous Overland Track takes on a new allure as the landscapes are painted with autumn hues.

Wine enthusiasts will find autumn particularly delightful as it coincides with the grape harvest season. The Tamar Valley, renowned for its vineyards, offers wine tastings amid stunning autumn landscapes.

Winter (June to August):

Winter in Tasmania brings a different kind of beauty. While the temperatures drop, snow blankets the higher elevations, creating a winter wonderland. Cradle Mountain and Mount Wellington become popular destinations for snow enthusiasts, offering opportunities for skiing, snowboarding, and simply enjoying the snowy landscapes.

Winter is also an excellent time for indulging in Tasmania's culinary delights. Cozy up in front of a fireplace in one of the island's charming cottages and savor local produce and wines.

Spring (September to November):

As winter bids farewell, Tasmania blossoms into life once again during spring. Blooms of wildflowers and cherry blossoms adorn the landscapes, and the air is filled with a sense of renewal. Spring is an ideal time for nature walks and bird watching as the island's wildlife becomes more active.

The mild temperatures make spring a comfortable time for exploring both urban and rural areas. Visit Hobart and Launceston to experience the cultural scene, attend festivals, and explore the burgeoning food culture.

The best time to visit Tasmania depends on your preferences and the type of experience you seek. Whether you're drawn to the lively summer atmosphere, the stunning autumn foliage, the winter snowscapes, or the blossoming landscapes of spring, Tasmania has something to offer year-round. Each season brings its own magic to this island paradise, ensuring that anytime you choose to visit, you'll be treated to a unique and unforgettable experience.

Duration of Stay

For those yearning for a taste of Tasmania's main highlights, a week-long stay could be ideal. This timeframe allows you to explore key regions, immerse yourself in the cultural hubs, and indulge in some of the island's renowned culinary delights. Hobart, the capital city, deserves a couple of days for its historic sites, vibrant markets, and the iconic MONA (Museum of Old and New Art). Moving north, Launceston, with its charming Cataract Gorge and surrounding wineries, is another must-visit city.

The allure of Tasmania extends bey"nd its urban centers. Nature enthusiasts will find solace in the island's national parks, each offering a unique blend of flora and fauna. Cradle Mountain-Lake St Clair National Park, a UNESCO World Heritage site, demands at least a day for those seeking to conquer its iconic peaks or simply revel in its breathtaking landscapes. Similarly, the Freycinet Peninsula on the east coast, with its pristine beaches and the renowned Wineglass Bay, deserves dedicated exploration time.

However, for a more immersive experience, extending your stay to ten days or more unveils Tasmania's hidden gems. Delve deeper into the lesser-explored regions, such as the rugged West Coast or the untouched wilderness of Southwest National Park. Such an extended stay allows for spontaneous detours, meandering through charming towns, and discovering local stories that enrich the overall travel experience.

Photography enthusiasts and outdoor adventurers may find that a longer stay allows them to capture the essence of Tasmania's diverse environments. From the white sandy beaches of the Bay of Fires to the jagged cliffs of Cape Raoul, the island's landscapes offer a myriad of photo opportunities that unveil themselves at different times of the day.

For those seeking a more leisurely pace, a fortnight in Tasmania opens the door to a more profound connection with the island. Take the time to engage with the locals, savoring the slower rhythm of life in smaller communities. Attend local events and festivals, where the island's rich cultural heritage comes to life, and you become more than just a spectator—you become part of the tapestry of Tasmania.

It's worth noting that Tasmania's weather can be unpredictable, with the island experiencing four distinct seasons. Allowing for a more extended stay provides flexibility to adapt your plans based on weather conditions, ensuring you don't miss out on any outdoor adventures due to unexpected rain or storms.

The duration of your stay in Tasmania is a deeply personal choice, shaped by your interests and the depth of exploration you desire. Whether you're a whirlwind traveler seeking the highlights or a slow-paced wanderer aiming to uncover every nuance, Tasmania welcomes you with open arms, promising an experience that will linger in your memory long after you bid farewell to this island paradise.

GETTING THERE

Airlines Connecting You to Tasmania: A Comprehensive Guide

Accessible by air, the island-state is served by several reputable airlines, each offering a distinct travel experience. In this guide, we will delve into the airlines connecting you to Tasmania, exploring their services, routes, and what makes them stand out.

Virgin Australia

Virgin Australia is a prominent player in the aviation industry, connecting major cities in Australia to Tasmania. With its modern fleet and commitment to customer satisfaction, Virgin Australia provides a comfortable and reliable journey. The airline offers daily flights to Hobart and Launceston, making it a convenient choice for both business and leisure travelers.

Qantas Airways

As the flagship carrier of Australia, Qantas is synonymous with quality and efficiency. Qantas provides regular flights to Hobart and Launceston from key Australian cities. Travelers can enjoy a range of services, including in-flight entertainment and premium cabin options. QantasLink, the regional subsidiary of Qantas, also operates flights to smaller airports in Tasmania, enhancing accessibility.

Jetstar Airways

For budget-conscious travelers, Jetstar Airways is a popular choice. Known for its affordable fares, Jetstar offers a cost-effective way to reach Tasmania without compromising on essential services. The airline operates regular flights to Hobart and Launceston, making it an accessible option for those looking to explore Tasmania on a budget.

Regional Express (Rex)

Rex is a regional airline that connects smaller Australian towns to major cities. While not serving Tasmania directly, Rex offers connecting flights, providing a comprehensive travel network. Travelers from regional areas can seamlessly transfer onto Rex services to reach Tasmania, ensuring accessibility for those coming from less urbanized areas.

Tigerair Australia

Tigerair Australia, now a subsidiary of Virgin Australia, was known for its low-cost model. While Tigerair Australia no longer operates as a standalone airline, its legacy continues through Virgin Australia's commitment to providing affordable options. Travelers can benefit from competitive pricing on flights to Tasmania while enjoying the amenities of a major airline.

International Connections

Tasmania is not only accessible from within Australia but also through international connections. Airlines such as Singapore Airlines, Emirates, and Air New Zealand offer flights to major Australian cities with seamless connections to Tasmania. These international carriers provide a gateway for global travelers to explore the unique beauty of the island-state.

Unique Features and Services

Each airline brings its own set of features and services to the table. From loyalty programs to in-flight entertainment and dining options, travelers to Tasmania have a variety of choices. Qantas, for example, boasts its renowned Qantas Club, providing lounge access to eligible passengers, while Virgin Australia emphasizes its Velocity Frequent Flyer program.

Booking Tips and Considerations

When planning a trip to Tasmania, it's essential to consider factors such as booking flexibility, baggage policies, and potential layovers. Some airlines offer package deals that include accommodation and car rentals, providing a hassle-free experience for travelers. Additionally, keeping an eye on seasonal promotions and discounts can lead to significant cost savings.

Virgin Australia: Soaring to Tasmania's Tranquil Beauty

In the vast expanse of the Southern Hemisphere, Tasmania stands as a beacon of natural splendor. Known for its rugged landscapes, pristine wilderness, and unique wildlife, this Australian island-state has become a sought-after destination for travelers seeking an escape into nature's wonders. For those arriving by air, Virgin Australia has emerged as a key player, seamlessly connecting major cities to the picturesque airports of Hobart and Launceston. In this exploration, we delve into the nuances of Virgin Australia's services to Tasmania, unraveling the tapestry of convenience, comfort, and commitment that defines the airline's journey to this island gem.

Virgin Australia, established in 2000 as Virgin Blue, has undergone significant transformations over the years. From its humble beginnings as a low-cost carrier, it has evolved into a full-service airline with a modern fleet and a commitment to providing a comprehensive travel experience. The airline's foray into Tasmania reflects not only the island's growing popularity but also Virgin Australia's strategic approach to catering to diverse traveler needs.

The airline operates daily flights to both Hobart and Launceston, ensuring that passengers have ample options to plan their journey. The frequency of flights underscores Virgin Australia's dedication to facilitating travel to Tasmania, recognizing the island's unique allure as a destination that combines outdoor adventure, cultural richness, and historical significance.

Virgin Australia's flights to Tasmania primarily depart from major Australian cities such as Sydney, Melbourne, and Brisbane. These key departure points act as gateways, allowing travelers from various parts of the country to seamlessly connect to the island-state. The convenience of having multiple departure cities enhances accessibility for a broad spectrum of travelers, whether they are embarking on a family vacation, a solo adventure, or a business trip.

The in-flight experience with Virgin Australia is marked by a blend of modern amenities and a focus on passenger comfort. Travelers can expect a range of seating options, from economy to business class, each designed to cater to different preferences and budgets. The airline's commitment to providing a comfortable journey extends beyond seating arrangements, encompassing in-flight entertainment, complimentary meals and beverages, and attentive cabin crew service.

Virgin Australia's Velocity Frequent Flyer program is an integral part of the airline's appeal. Designed to reward loyal customers, the program offers a range of benefits, including points accrual, lounge access, and exclusive perks. For travelers who frequently journey to Tasmania or other destinations serviced by Virgin Australia, the Velocity Frequent Flyer program adds an extra layer of value to their flying experience.

When travelers choose Virgin Australia to reach Tasmania, they not only benefit from the airline's commitment to service excellence but also from its focus on operational reliability. Punctuality and adherence to schedules are critical aspects of the airline industry, and Virgin Australia takes pride in its track record of timely departures and arrivals. This reliability is particularly crucial for those with tight itineraries or connecting flights, providing peace of mind as they traverse the skies to Tasmania.

As a full-service airline, Virgin Australia extends its commitment to customer satisfaction to the ground as well. From user-friendly online booking platforms to efficient check-in processes, the airline strives to make the entire travel experience seamless and stress-free. The integration of technology and customer service excellence ensures that passengers can navigate their journey effortlessly, from the moment they decide to explore Tasmania to the time they set foot on the island.

Beyond the functional aspects of air travel, Virgin Australia recognizes the environmental responsibilities that come with operating in the modern world. The airline has implemented initiatives to reduce its carbon footprint, contributing to the broader industry's efforts to address sustainability concerns. For travelers conscious of their environmental impact, choosing an airline with a commitment to eco-friendly practices adds an extra layer of significance to their journey.

Tasmania, with its diverse landscapes and unique attractions, beckons travelers to explore its wonders. The partnership between Virgin Australia and Tasmania goes beyond mere transportation; it is a bridge that connects eager adventurers to the island's tranquility. As travelers embark on a Virgin Australia flight bound for Hobart or Launceston, they are not just passengers; they are participants in a journey that promises discovery, relaxation, and a deep connection with one of Australia's most captivating destinations.

Virgin Australia's role in connecting travelers to Tasmania is more than a logistical one. It is a commitment to facilitating experiences, forging memories, and enabling a seamless transition from the bustling mainland to the serene landscapes of Tasmania. Whether you are gazing at the panoramic views from the plane's window or relishing the in-flight amenities, the journey with Virgin Australia becomes an integral part of the overall adventure—a prelude to the enchanting escapades awaiting in the heart of Australia's island paradise.

Qantas Airways: A Journey to Tasmania's Gateway

Tasmania beckons travelers with its pristine landscapes, rich history, and unique wildlife. As one of Australia's most sought-after destinations, accessing this island-state is made seamless and comfortable through various airlines. Among them, Qantas Airways stands out as a beacon of reliability, comfort, and a commitment to delivering a world-class travel experience. In this exploration, we delve into the nuances of Qantas Airways and the journey it offers to Tasmania.

Qantas, the iconic flag carrier of Australia, has long been synonymous with air travel excellence. With a history spanning over a century, the airline has earned a reputation for safety, punctuality, and a dedication to passenger satisfaction. For those seeking a journey to Tasmania, Qantas presents an array of services and features that make the voyage not just a means of transportation but an integral part of the overall travel experience.

Tasmania, with its capital city Hobart and other key destinations like Launceston, Cradle Mountain, and the Freycinet Peninsula, is well-connected to major Australian cities through Qantas. The airline's extensive domestic network ensures that travelers can seamlessly reach Tasmania from cities such as Sydney, Melbourne, Brisbane, and Adelaide. This accessibility has played a pivotal role in Tasmania's emergence as a must-visit destination for both domestic and international tourists.

One of the standout features of Qantas is its commitment to providing a range of services catering to different passenger needs. The airline offers various travel classes, including Economy, Premium Economy, Business, and First Class. Each class is designed to provide a distinct level of comfort, ensuring that passengers can tailor their journey according to their preferences and budget.

The Economy Class of Qantas is far from basic, offering a comfortable and spacious environment for travelers. Passengers can enjoy complimentary meals, snacks, and beverages during their flight, along with a selection of entertainment options to make the journey more enjoyable. The ergonomically designed seats and attentive cabin crew contribute to a positive flying experience, making the journey to Tasmania a pleasant one.

For those seeking an extra level of comfort without the premium cost, Qantas offers Premium Economy. This class provides larger seats with increased recline, enhanced meal options, and a dedicated cabin crew, allowing passengers to arrive at their destination feeling refreshed and relaxed. It's a middle ground between the economy and business classes, providing a taste of luxury without breaking the bank.

Business Class on Qantas is synonymous with sophistication and pampering. Passengers in this class enjoy priority check-in, access to Qantas lounges, and spacious seats that can transform into fully-flat beds. The culinary offerings in Business Class are curated by renowned chefs, ensuring a gourmet dining experience at 30,000 feet. The comprehensive in-flight entertainment system and amenity kits further elevate the travel experience.

For the epitome of luxury, Qantas offers First Class service on selected international routes. While direct First Class flights to Tasmania may not be available, passengers can experience the pinnacle of air travel luxury when flying internationally with Qantas. First Class cabins boast private suites, exquisite dining options, premium wines, and a dedicated cabin crew, providing an unparalleled level of comfort and service.

QantasLink, the regional subsidiary of Qantas, extends the airline's reach to smaller airports and communities. While not all QantasLink flights directly connect to Tasmania, they play a crucial role in connecting regional areas to major cities, providing a comprehensive travel network for those venturing to the island-state.

One of the distinctive features of Qantas is its commitment to sustainability and responsible flying. The airline has implemented various initiatives to reduce its environmental impact, including investments in fuel-efficient aircraft, waste reduction programs, and carbon offset options for passengers. This aligns with the growing awareness and concern for sustainable travel practices, making Qantas an appealing choice for environmentally conscious travelers.

When planning a journey with Qantas to Tasmania, there are practical considerations that can enhance the overall experience. Booking flexibility, baggage allowances, and potential layovers are essential factors to consider. Qantas often provides package deals that include accommodation and car rentals, streamlining the travel process and offering convenience to passengers.

Qantas Airways serves as a gateway to Tasmania, offering a seamless and comfortable journey to this enchanting island-state. Whether you're an economy traveler seeking affordability or a business-class passenger in pursuit of luxury, Qantas provides a spectrum of options to cater to diverse preferences. With a focus on safety, sustainability, and passenger satisfaction, Qantas continues to be a trusted choice for those embarking on a journey to discover the natural wonders and cultural richness of Tasmania. As you step on board a Qantas flight bound for Tasmania, you're not just flying; you're embarking on an experience that complements the adventure that awaits on the island's shores.

Jetstar Airways: Your Gateway to Tasmania

Jetstar Airways, a prominent player in the budget airline sector, has become a popular choice for travelers seeking affordable and convenient options to explore the diverse landscapes of Tasmania. In this comprehensive exploration, we delve into the key aspects of Jetstar's services to Tasmania, ranging from its route network and fleet to the in-flight experience and the unique features that set it apart in the competitive aviation industry.

Founded in 2003 as a subsidiary of Qantas, Jetstar quickly carved a niche for itself by focusing on low-cost travel without compromising on safety or customer satisfaction. As part of the Qantas Group, Jetstar operates as a value-based carrier, providing an extensive network within Australia and across the Asia-Pacific region. For those planning a trip to Tasmania, Jetstar stands out as an accessible and budget-friendly option.

Jetstar Airways operates regular flights to two primary destinations in Tasmania: Hobart and Launceston. These cities serve as key entry points for travelers looking to explore the island's rich natural beauty, historical sites, and vibrant culture. The airline's strategic focus on connecting major Australian cities to Tasmania enhances accessibility for both domestic and international travelers.

The routes to Hobart and Launceston cover major airports such as Sydney, Melbourne, Brisbane, and Adelaide, ensuring a wide range of departure points for those planning a Tasmanian adventure. Jetstar's commitment to providing direct and efficient connections aligns with the preferences of budget-conscious travelers who value both time and affordability.

Jetstar maintains a modern fleet of Airbus A320 and Boeing 787 Dreamliner aircraft, contributing to a reliable and efficient travel experience. The Airbus A320, known for its fuel efficiency and environmental performance, is a workhorse for short to medium-haul flights, making it an ideal choice for travel to Tasmania. The Boeing 787 Dreamliner, with its long-range capabilities, further extends Jetstar's reach across the Asia-Pacific region.

The airline's commitment to a well-maintained and technologically advanced fleet reflects its dedication to passenger safety and comfort. Travelers choosing Jetstar can expect a smooth and reliable journey aboard these state-of-the-art aircraft.

One of Jetstar's primary appeals is its commitment to providing affordable travel options. The airline adopts a transparent pricing model, allowing passengers to choose additional services based on their preferences. From seat selection to in-flight meals, Jetstar's à la carte approach empowers travelers to tailor their journey to suit their needs and budget.

The airline's competitive pricing strategies extend to regular promotions, sales, and package deals. Travelers keen on exploring Tasmania without breaking the bank often find Jetstar's offerings attractive. The combination of cost-effective base fares and the flexibility to customize the travel experience positions Jetstar as a top choice for those seeking value for money.

While Jetstar positions itself as a budget airline, it doesn't compromise on essential in-flight services. Passengers traveling to Tasmania with Jetstar can expect a comfortable journey with standard amenities, including in-flight entertainment options, refreshments, and the opportunity to purchase additional snacks and beverages.

Jetstar's commitment to customer satisfaction is evident in its friendly cabin crew and a focus on maintaining cleanliness and hygiene. Despite its budget-friendly approach, Jetstar aims to ensure a positive and enjoyable in-flight experience for all passengers, contributing to the overall appeal of choosing the airline for your journey to Tasmania.

Booking a flight with Jetstar is a straightforward process, thanks to its user-friendly website and mobile app. Travelers can easily navigate through the booking platform, select their preferred flights, and customize their experience based on personal preferences. Jetstar's commitment to digital innovation ensures a seamless online booking process.

When planning a trip to Tasmania with Jetstar, consider booking in advance to take advantage of lower base fares. Additionally, keep an eye out for promotional periods and sales, as Jetstar frequently offers discounts on selected routes. While budget-conscious travelers appreciate the standard offerings, such as the 7kg carry-on baggage allowance, it's advisable to review the baggage policies and consider any additional services needed for a more tailored travel experience.

In recent years, environmental sustainability has become a key focus for many industries, including aviation. Jetstar has taken steps to address its environmental impact through initiatives aimed at reducing carbon emissions and promoting eco-friendly practices. The airline invests in fuel-efficient aircraft, explores sustainable aviation fuels, and actively participates in programs to offset carbon emissions.

As travelers become increasingly conscious of the environmental impact of their journeys, Jetstar's commitment to sustainability aligns with the values of those seeking responsible travel options. Choosing Jetstar for your trip to Tasmania allows you to contribute to a more environmentally friendly aviation industry.

Jetstar Airways emerges as a compelling choice for travelers embarking on a journey to Tasmania. With its expansive route network, modern fleet, and commitment to affordability, Jetstar caters to a diverse audience seeking a budget-friendly and accessible travel experience. The airline's in-flight services and environmental initiatives further enhance its appeal, making it a top choice for those who value a balance between cost, comfort, and sustainability.

Whether you're a solo adventurer, a budget-conscious family, or a group of friends looking to explore the wonders of Tasmania, Jetstar provides a gateway to this captivating island. By combining convenience, affordability, and a commitment to customer satisfaction, Jetstar Airways stands out as a reliable partner for your Tasmanian adventure, ensuring that your journey is as memorable as the destination itself.

Regional Express (Rex)

Regional Express (Rex), a stalwart in Australia's regional aviation landscape, stands out as a key player connecting smaller communities across the country. While Rex doesn't directly serve Tasmania, its significance lies in its extensive regional network, providing vital air links to communities that may otherwise be isolated. In this comprehensive exploration, we delve into the intricacies of Rex's operations, its role in regional connectivity, and how travelers can leverage its services to reach the picturesque island-state of Tasmania.

Rex, founded in 2002, has firmly established itself as a reliable regional airline. The airline's primary mission is to connect regional and remote communities, fostering economic development and ensuring access to essential services. Operating on a foundation of safety, reliability, and community engagement, Rex has become a trusted name in the regional aviation sector.

Rex's network extends to various regional destinations across Australia, covering routes that are often crucial lifelines for the communities they serve. While Rex doesn't operate direct flights to Tasmania, its extensive network indirectly facilitates travel to the island by providing connections to major airports.

For travelers aiming to reach Tasmania via Rex, the journey typically involves a two-step process. First, passengers would take a Rex flight from a regional airport to a major hub, such as Sydney, Melbourne, or Adelaide. From there, they can seamlessly transfer to another airline, like Qantas or Virgin Australia, offering direct flights to Tasmania.

This indirect route to Tasmania showcases the importance of Rex in enabling connectivity for passengers from regional areas. It not only enhances accessibility for residents of smaller towns and cities but also contributes to the broader tourism landscape by linking tourists to popular destinations like Tasmania.

Rex operates a fleet of Saab 340 aircraft, known for their reliability and suitability for regional routes. These planes are designed to navigate shorter runways, making them well-suited for erving airports in smaller communities. The airline's commitment to safety and operational fficiency is reflected in its choice of aircraft and rigorous maintenance standards.

assengers traveling with Rex to connect to Tasmania can expect a no-frills, efficient flying xperience. The airline focuses on the essentials, ensuring that regional flights are punctual, eliable, and affordable. While the amenities may not rival those of larger carriers, Rex's mphasis on safety and reliability makes it a preferred choice for those traveling to and from egional areas.

he airline's contribution to regional connectivity goes beyond passenger services. Rex also perates freight services, transporting goods and mail to remote locations. This dual role as oth a passenger and freight carrier underscores Rex's integral position in supporting regional conomies and maintaining essential links between communities.

 recent years, Rex has expanded its operations and ventured into new markets, signaling a ommitment to growth and adaptability. While Tasmania may not currently be directly served y Rex, ongoing developments in the aviation industry suggest that regional connectivity, cluding potential routes to Tasmania, could evolve in the future.

or travelers considering Rex as part of their journey to Tasmania, it's essential to plan arefully, taking into account layover times and potential schedule changes. Coordinating Rex ights with connecting services to Tasmania requires careful consideration of flight schedules nd ensuring sufficient time for transfers.

egional Express (Rex) plays a pivotal role in Australia's regional aviation landscape, connecting naller communities and fostering economic development. While Rex doesn't operate direct ights to Tasmania, its extensive regional network indirectly facilitates travel to the island by roviding crucial connections to major airports. The airline's commitment to safety, reliability, nd community engagement positions it as a key player in enhancing accessibility for regional esidents and contributing to the broader tourism landscape. As travelers explore the unique eauty of Tasmania, the indirect journey facilitated by Rex serves as a testament to the airline's ɔle in connecting Australia's diverse regions.

igerair Australia: A Gateway to Tasmania's Wonders

 the realm of budget-friendly air travel, Tigerair Australia has carved a niche for itself, offering ffordable options without compromising on essential services. For travelers seeking an conomical yet comfortable journey to Tasmania, Tigerair Australia presents a compelling choice. In this exploration, we delve into the airline's offerings, its routes to Tasmania, and the unique features that set it apart.

Tigerair Australia, formerly an independent low-cost carrier, has been a significant player in the Australian aviation landscape. While it no longer operates as a standalone entity, its legacy persists under the wing of Virgin Australia. As a subsidiary of Virgin Australia, Tigerair's commitment to providing cost-effective travel options aligns with Virgin's broader strategy of catering to diverse passenger needs.

One of the primary draws of Tigerair Australia is its focus on affordability. The airline is well-known for offering competitive fares, making it an attractive option for travelers with budget constraints. With Tasmania emerging as a sought-after destination for nature enthusiasts, Tigerair's cost-effective model becomes particularly appealing, allowing a broader demographic to explore the island's natural wonders.

Tigerair Australia primarily serves two major airports in Tasmania – Hobart and Launceston. These airports act as gateways to the island's diverse landscapes, from the bustling cultural scenes of Hobart to the pristine wilderness around Launceston. The airline operates regular flights to and from these key Tasmanian cities, facilitating convenient travel for both locals and tourists alike.

The airline's commitment to accessibility is further emphasized by its network of routes within mainland Australia. Travelers from various cities can seamlessly connect to Tigerair Australia's services, creating a comprehensive travel network. While the airline may not boast an extensive global reach, its focus on domestic connections ensures that Tasmania remains within easy reach for a wide audience.

An essential aspect of any airline's appeal Is the overall travel experience it provides. Tigerair Australia, despite its emphasis on affordability, strives to offer a comfortable and enjoyable journey. Modern and well-maintained aircraft contribute to a sense of reliability, assuring passengers that they can reach their destination safely. The airline's commitment to safety standards aligns with industry regulations, providing peace of mind for those on board.

In-flight services play a crucial role in shaping the passenger experience, and Tigerair Australia no stranger to this reality. While the airline may not offer the extensive in-flight amenities found in premium carriers, it does provide essential services to ensure a comfortable journey. Onboard refreshments, comfortable seating, and friendly cabin crew contribute to a positive atmosphere, allowing passengers to focus on the excitement of reaching their Tasmanian destination.

For travelers unfamiliar with the intricacies of budget airlines, it's essential to understand Tigerair Australia's approach to ancillary services. The airline often adopts a "pay-as-you-go" model, where passengers can choose to pay for additional services based on their preferences.

From seat selection to extra baggage allowances, these add-on options provide flexibility, allowing travelers to tailor their experience according to their needs and budget.

As Tigerair Australia operates under the umbrella of Virgin Australia, passengers can also benefit from certain synergies between the two airlines. This collaboration extends to loyalty programs, where passengers can earn and redeem points through Virgin Australia's Velocity Frequent Flyer program. For frequent travelers, this integration provides an opportunity to accrue rewards and enjoy additional perks, enhancing the overall value proposition.

While Tigerair Australia is a popular choice for those seeking affordable travel, it's crucial for passengers to be aware of the airline's policies and limitations. Budget carriers often have stricter rules regarding baggage allowances, check-in procedures, and modifications to bookings. Understanding these aspects beforehand can help travelers navigate the experience more smoothly and avoid any unexpected challenges.

Tigerair Australia stands as a gateway to Tasmania, offering an accessible and budget-friendly means of reaching this captivating island destination. While it may not provide the lavish amenities associated with premium carriers, its commitment to affordability and safety makes it a compelling choice for a broad spectrum of travelers. As Tasmania continues to beckon with its natural beauty and cultural richness, Tigerair Australia ensures that the journey is as memorable as the destination itself. So, whether you're a budget-conscious adventurer or a seasoned traveler seeking new horizons, consider Tigerair Australia as your conduit to the wonders of Tasmania.

Navigating Tasmania's Waters: A Guide to the Best Ferry Services

Exploring this picturesque destination is made all the more convenient and scenic with the availability of ferry services. In this guide, we delve into the best ferry services in Tasmania, offering travelers an alternative means of transportation to unlock the island's hidden gems.

1. Spirit of Tasmania

Undoubtedly the most iconic ferry service in Tasmania, the Spirit of Tasmania has been connecting the mainland (Melbourne) to Devonport since 1985. The journey unfolds over the Bass Strait, providing passengers with breathtaking views of the coastline. With both day and night sailings, travelers can choose between a relaxing daytime voyage or an overnight experience, arriving in Tasmania refreshed and ready to explore. Onboard amenities include comfortable cabins, dining options, and entertainment, ensuring a seamless and enjoyable journey.

2. Bruny Island Ferry

For those looking to explore the natural beauty of Bruny Island, the Bruny Island Ferry is an essential transport link. Operating between Kettering on the mainland and Roberts Point on Bruny Island, this short but scenic journey immerses passengers in the stunning waters of the D'Entrecasteaux Channel. The ferry accommodates both vehicles and foot passengers, making it a versatile choice for travelers seeking to experience the untouched landscapes and wildlife of Bruny Island.

3. Maria Island Ferry

Accessing the serene Maria Island, a UNESCO World Heritage-listed site, is made possible by the Maria Island Ferry. Departing from Triabunna, this ferry service provides a gateway to a unique blend of history, wildlife, and natural beauty. Visitors can explore convict-era ruins, encounter native wildlife, and embark on hiking trails that showcase the island's diverse ecosystems. With regular departures, the Maria Island Ferry facilitates day trips or extended stays, catering to the varied preferences of travelers.

4. Peppermint Bay Cruise

While not a traditional ferry service, the Peppermint Bay Cruise offers a luxurious and scenic journey from Hobart to the charming Peppermint Bay. This cruise provides a unique perspective of the Derwent River, framed by lush landscapes and historic sites. Travelers can indulge in gourmet dining onboard, savoring Tasmania's renowned culinary delights. The Peppermint Bay Cruise is a perfect blend of transportation and gastronomic experience, making it an attractive option for those seeking a more leisurely journey.

Tasmania's ferry services are not merely a means of transportation; they are gateways to adventure, allowing travelers to immerse themselves in the island's diverse landscapes and attractions. Whether embarking on the Spirit of Tasmania for a mainland connection or exploring the island's coastal gems with specialized ferries, these services contribute to the unique charm of Tasmania as a travel destination. Embrace the allure of Tasmania's waters and let the ferry services pave the way for unforgettable experiences.

The Spirit of Tasmania: Navigating the Seas to Tasmania's Heart

The Spirit of Tasmania stands as an iconic maritime link, connecting the mainland of Australia to the picturesque island state of Tasmania. Since its inaugural journey in 1985, this ferry service has become synonymous with the exploration of Tasmania's diverse landscapes, creating a unique and memorable travel experience for thousands of passengers annually.

The Spirit of Tasmania operates between Melbourne on the Australian mainland and Devonport on the northern coast of Tasmania. The journey unfolds across the Bass Strait, a stretch of water that, while notoriously challenging, adds an element of adventure to the travel experience. The two vessels, Spirit of Tasmania I and Spirit of Tasmania II, were introduced in 1998 and 2002, respectively, enhancing the capacity and comfort of the service.

One of the undeniable highlights of the Spirit of Tasmania journey is the opportunity to witness breathtaking coastal scenery. As the ferry departs from Melbourne's Station Pier, passengers are treated to panoramic views of the city skyline before the landscape gradually transitions to the open waters of the Bass Strait. The sunset vistas over the ocean provide a serene and awe-inspiring spectacle, creating a fitting introduction to the natural beauty that awaits in Tasmania.

The Spirit of Tasmania offers both day and night sailings, providing travelers with the flexibility to choose a schedule that aligns with their preferences and itineraries. The day sailing option allows passengers to revel in the sunlight, enjoying the expansive views and onboard amenities. On the other hand, night sailings provide a unique experience as passengers can witness the sunrise over the Tasmanian coastline, signaling the beginning of a new day of exploration.

To ensure a comfortable and enjoyable journey, the Spirit of Tasmania is equipped with a range of onboard amenities. Travelers can choose from various cabin options, from standard cabins to deluxe cabins with private facilities. The vessels feature lounges, bars, and restaurants, offering a selection of meals and beverages. The onboard entertainment options cater to diverse preferences, making the ferry journey an integral part of the overall travel experience.

The Spirit of Tasmania accommodates not only foot passengers but also vehicles, including cars, campervans, and motorcycles. This makes it an ideal choice for travelers seeking the flexibility of bringing their vehicles to explore Tasmania at their own pace. The convenience of transporting vehicles also contributes to the ferry's popularity among both tourists and locals, enhancing the accessibility of Tasmania's attractions.

For those opting for the night sailing experience, the Spirit of Tasmania offers the convenience of onboard cabins, allowing passengers to rest and rejuvenate during the voyage. The cabins are

well-appointed, providing a comfortable retreat with bedding, bathroom facilities, and the gentle rocking motion of the ferry contributing to a peaceful night's sleep. This unique overnight experience adds an extra layer of adventure to the journey, transforming it into a seamless transition from one destination to another.

Beyond its role as a mode of transportation for travelers, the Spirit of Tasmania plays a vital role in connecting communities. The ferry service facilitates the movement of goods and supplies between the mainland and Tasmania, contributing to the economic well-being of the island. Additionally, it serves as a lifeline for residents, ensuring a reliable link to the broader Australian infrastructure.

The Spirit of Tasmania is not merely a ferry service; it is an integral part of Tasmania's tourism industry. As the primary maritime route to the island, the ferry welcomes visitors with a sense of anticipation, setting the tone for the adventures that lie ahead. The journey itself becomes a memorable chapter in the travel narrative, with passengers forming lasting impressions of Tasmania from the moment they step onboard.

In recent years, there has been a growing awareness of the environmental impact of transportation, and the maritime industry is no exception. The Spirit of Tasmania has taken steps to address these concerns, incorporating sustainable practices to reduce its ecological footprint. From waste management initiatives to fuel efficiency measures, the ferry service demonstrates a commitment to responsible travel, ensuring that the pristine natural environment of Tasmania is preserved for future generations.

The Spirit of Tasmania is more than a vessel navigating the waters between Melbourne and Devonport; it is a gateway to the heart of Tasmania. Its significance goes beyond the practicalities of transportation, encompassing the thrill of exploration, the beauty of the sea, and the seamless connection of two distinct lands. For those embarking on this maritime journey, the Spirit of Tasmania weaves itself into the fabric of their Tasmanian adventure, creating memories that endure long after the ferry docks at its destination.

Bruny Island Ferry: Navigating the D'Entrecasteaux Channel

The allure of Tasmania lies not only in its mainland wonders but also in the hidden gems scattered across its surrounding islands. One such gem is Bruny Island, a haven of natural beauty, rugged coastlines, and unique wildlife. Accessible by sea, the Bruny Island Ferry stands as a vital link between the mainland and this pristine island sanctuary. As the vessel glides across the D'Entrecasteaux Channel, it unveils not just a mode of transportation but an integral part of the Tasmanian experience.

The Bruny Island Ferry operates between Kettering, a small town on the mainland, and Roberts Point on Bruny Island. This short but picturesque journey encapsulates the essence of Tasmania's coastal beauty, making it an essential element of any traveler's itinerary.

The ferry voyage begins at Kettering, a coastal village located approximately 30 kilometers south of Hobart. Nestled along the shores of the D'Entrecasteaux Channel, Kettering is not only the departure point for the Bruny Island Ferry but also a charming destination in its own right. Travelers often find solace in the tranquility of Kettering, taking in the sea breeze and enjoying the coastal views before embarking on their Bruny Island adventure.

As the ferry departs from Kettering, passengers are treated to panoramic views of the D'Entrecasteaux Channel. The channel, named after French explorer Bruni d'Entrecasteaux, separates Bruny Island from the Tasmanian mainland. The deep blue waters stretch out, framed by rolling hills and occasional glimpses of marine life. Seabirds dance in the air, creating a lively spectacle against the backdrop of the open sea.

The journey is not just a means of transportation but an experience in itself. Travelers have the option to embark on the ferry with their vehicles, adding a layer of convenience for those looking to explore Bruny Island at their own pace. The seamless transition from the mainland to the island is a testament to the engineering marvel that is the Bruny Island Ferry.

As the ferry approaches Roberts Point on Bruny Island, anticipation builds among passengers. Roberts Point serves as the gateway to the island's southern region, where natural wonders and cultural heritage converge. The ferry docks, and passengers disembark onto Bruny Island, greeted by the untouched landscapes that define this corner of Tasmania.

Bruny Island's appeal lies in its unspoiled wilderness. Travelers can explore the diverse ecosystems, from the towering cliffs of Cape Bruny to the serene beaches of Adventure Bay. The island is a haven for birdwatchers, with rare species like the endangered forty-spotted pardalote finding refuge in its habitats. The South Bruny National Park, covering a significant portion of the island, invites hikers to traverse its trails and discover the unique flora and fauna that call Bruny home.

History enthusiasts are not left wanting on Bruny Island. The Cape Bruny Lighthouse, standing proudly since 1838, provides a glimpse into Tasmania's maritime past. The island's convict history is revealed through structures like the remains of the old Lunawanna convict station, adding a layer of intrigue to the exploration of Bruny's landscapes.

The Bruny Island Ferry operates at regular intervals, allowing for day trips or extended stays on the island. This flexibility accommodates the diverse preferences of travelers, whether they seek a brief escape from the mainland or an immersive experience in Bruny's natural wonders.

The journey back to Kettering is, in many ways, a reflection on the experiences gained on Bruny Island. As the ferry retraces its path across the D'Entrecasteaux Channel, passengers can savor the memories created on the island – the taste of fresh oysters, the sound of waves crashing against the cliffs, and the sight of Bruny's unique wildlife.

The Bruny Island Ferry is not merely a transportation link; it's a vessel that connects travelers to the soul of Tasmania. It seamlessly integrates the mainland with the island, allowing visitors to experience the raw beauty of Bruny's landscapes. As the ferry departs from Kettering and arrives at Roberts Point, it signifies not just a change in location but a transition into the untamed allure of Bruny Island, where every wave carries the whispers of Tasmania's natural wonders.

Maria Island Ferry: Gateway to Tranquility and Natural Splendor

Tasmania, an island state known for its breathtaking landscapes and unique wildlife, offers a myriad of destinations that beckon to be explored. One such gem is Maria Island, a pristine sanctuary boasting a rich tapestry of history, diverse ecosystems, and unparalleled beauty. Accessible primarily by the Maria Island Ferry, this mode of transportation serves as the gateway to an island that seamlessly intertwines the remnants of its convict past with the untouched allure of its natural surroundings.

The Maria Island Ferry operates from the quaint town of Triabunna, nestled along Tasmania's scenic east coast. Triabunna itself is a charming destination, and as visitors await their ferry, they are treated to views of the surrounding azure waters and the promise of the adventure that awaits. The ferry ride is not merely a means of transport; it is an integral part of the Maria Island experience, offering passengers a preview of the unspoiled landscapes that make this island a haven for nature enthusiasts.

Departing from Triabunna, the ferry journey unfolds across the Mercury Passage, a stretch of water that separates the mainland from Maria Island. The azure waters provide a serene backdrop, and as the ferry glides over the gentle waves, passengers are greeted by panoramic views of the Tasmanian coastline. The journey itself is a tranquil escape, setting the tone for the peaceful retreat that Maria Island promises.

As the ferry approaches the island, passengers are greeted by the iconic silhouette of the Painted Cliffs, a natural wonder that showcases the geological artistry of nature. The cliffs, adorned with vibrant mineral patterns, stand as a testament to the island's geological history and add a touch of magic to the arrival at Maria Island. The ferry docks at Darlington, Maria Island's main settlement, where history and nature converge to create an immersive and enriching experience.

Darlington, a former convict settlement, echoes with the whispers of the past. The haunting beauty of the preserved convict-era buildings stands in stark contrast to the untouched wilderness that surrounds them. Visitors can embark on a journey through time as they explore the Darlington Probation Station and other historical sites, gaining insights into the harsh realities faced by the convicts who once called Maria Island home.

Beyond its historical significance, Maria Island is a haven for wildlife enthusiasts and nature lovers. The island is a Noah's Ark of sorts, providing a sanctuary for endangered species and a habitat for a diverse array of fauna. Wombats wander freely, kangaroos graze in open meadows, and a plethora of bird species call the island home. The Fossil Cliffs, another geological marvel, offers a glimpse into the ancient marine life that once thrived in these waters, adding an extra layer of fascination for those interested in paleontology.

The Maria Island Ferry, with its regular departures from Triabunna, makes exploring this natural wonderland accessible to day-trippers and those seeking a more extended escape alike. Day-trippers can revel in the beauty of Maria Island's highlights, from the Painted Cliffs to the convict-era ruins, while those opting for a more leisurely stay can partake in the island's hiking trails, camping opportunities, and secluded beaches.

The allure of Maria Island extends beyond its daylight charm. The island is renowned for its pristine night skies, offering stargazers an unobstructed view of the southern celestial wonders. Camping under the starlit sky becomes a transformative experience, connecting visitors with the vastness of the universe and the untamed beauty of Maria Island.

The Maria Island Ferry service enhances the overall experience by not only providing transportation but by becoming an integral part of the island narrative. The friendly and knowledgeable staff on board often share insights into the island's history, ecology, and points of interest, enriching the journey with a deeper understanding of this unique Tasmanian destination.

The Maria Island Ferry is more than a vessel transporting visitors to and from an island; it is a conduit to a realm where history, nature, and tranquility converge. Maria Island, with its pristine landscapes and historical echoes, invites travelers to step back in time and immerse themselves in the untouched beauty of Tasmania. As the ferry departs from Triabunna and approaches the shores of Maria Island, it sets the stage for an exploration that transcends the ordinary—an

exploration of an island that remains a testament to the unspoiled wonders of the natural world.

The Peppermint Bay Cruise: Sailing"into Tasmanian Elegance

Nestled in the embrace of the Southern Ocean, Tasmania beckons travelers with its rugged coastlines, pristine wilderness, and a culinary scene that rivals the best in the world. Among the myriad ways to explore this island paradise, the Peppermint Bay Cruise stands out as a unique and luxurious experience, seamlessly blending maritime adventure with gourmet indulgence.

As the sun-drenched shores of Hobart unfold, the Peppermint Bay Cruise sets the stage for an unforgettable journey along the Derwent River. Departing from the historic Hobart waterfront, the vessel effortlessly glides through the tranquil waters, revealing a panorama of natural wonders and historic landmarks.

The Derwent River, with its deep blue waters and surrounding greenery, becomes the scenic canvas upon which the Peppermint Bay Cruise paints an immersive experience. The cruise not only serves as a means of transportation but also as a portal to a world where time seems to slow down, inviting passengers to savor every moment of the voyage.

One of the defining features of the Peppermint Bay Cruise is its commitment to providing a leisurely and indulgent experience. Passengers are treated to a luxurious setting, with spacious decks that allow for unobstructed views of the passing landscapes. Plush seating and attentive staff create an ambiance of comfort, ensuring that every traveler feels like a privileged guest.

As the cruise departs from Hobart, the journey unfolds with the iconic backdrop of the Tasman Bridge. This architectural marvel spans the Derwent River, connecting the eastern and western shores of Hobart. Passengers are treated to a unique perspective of this landmark, offering an ideal photo opportunity that encapsulates the spirit of Tasmania.

As the vessel navigates the river, passengers can witness a seamless blend of urbanity and nature. The shores are adorned with historic sites, including the remnants of the Female Factory, a stark reminder of Tasmania's convict past. The juxtaposition of the old and the new adds layers to the narrative, inviting travelers to reflect on the island's rich and complex history.

The Peppermint Bay Cruise is not merely a sightseeing adventure; it is a culinary journey that elevates the entire experience. Onboard, passengers are treated to a gastronomic extravaganza featuring Tasmania's renowned produce. The cruise boasts a gourmet restaurant where skilled chefs curate a menu that showcases the freshest local ingredients.

The voyage to Peppermint Bay unfolds gradually, allowing passengers to savor each course while taking in the mesmerizing views. Tasmanian seafood takes center stage, with dishes that celebrate the bounty of the surrounding waters. From succulent oysters to perfectly seared fish, every bite is a testament to the island's culinary prowess.

As the vessel approaches its destination, Peppermint Bay reveals itself as a picturesque enclave nestled along the D'Entrecasteaux Channel. Surrounded by rolling hills and azure waters, the bay exudes tranquility and natural beauty. Passengers disembark, stepping into a world where the charm of a coastal village meets the sophistication of a gourmet retreat.

Peppermint Bay itself is a destination worth exploring. The establishment, overlooking the bay, features a waterfront restaurant, showcasing the same commitment to culinary excellence as the cruise. The restaurant's expansive windows frame the breathtaking scenery, creating an atmosphere where diners can relish both the flavors on their plate and the views beyond.

For those seeking a more immersive experience, Peppermint Bay offers a variety of activities. Visitors can explore the nearby art galleries, stroll through the coastal gardens, or simply unwind on the pebble beaches that line the bay. The synergy between nature and human creativity is palpable, creating an ambiance that lingers in the memory long after the journey concludes.

The return leg of the Peppermint Bay Cruise allows passengers to bask in the afterglow of their onshore escapade. The journey back to Hobart becomes a reflective interlude, with the setting sun casting its golden hues upon the river. The landscape, though familiar, takes on a different allure as shadows lengthen, and the city lights begin to twinkle in the dusk.

As the Peppermint Bay Cruise docks back in Hobart, passengers disembark with a sense of fulfillment that goes beyond the typical travel experience. The cruise is not just a mode of transportation; it's a gateway to Tasmanian elegance, where the natural beauty of the surroundings is complemented by the sophistication of gourmet indulgence.

The Peppermint Bay Cruise transcends the traditional boundaries of maritime travel. It encapsulates the essence of Tasmania, offering a seamless blend of luxury, natural beauty, and culinary delights. For those seeking an immersive exploration of the island's coastal wonders, this cruise stands as a testament to Tasmania's ability to captivate the senses and leave an indelible mark on the hearts of those fortunate enough to embark on its journey.

HOBART

Overview of Hobart

Hobart, the capital city of Tasmania, Australia, is a captivating blend of rich history, modern culture, and stunning natural beauty. Nestled at the foot of Mount Wellington and bordered by the picturesque River Derwent, Hobart offers a unique experience for travelers seeking a perfect amalgamation of urban life and the tranquility of nature.

One of Hobart's defining features is its historic waterfront, where the iconic Salamanca Place stands as a testament to the city's maritime heritage. Cobblestone streets wind through this vibrant area, lined with 19th-century sandstone warehouses that have been repurposed into art galleries, boutiques, and cafes. On Saturdays, the Salamanca Market comes alive, attracting locals and visitors alike with its stalls selling everything from fresh produce to handmade crafts.

As you wander through the city, you'll encounter Battery Point, a charming neighborhood filled with well-preserved historic homes. Each building tells a story of Hobart's past, reflecting the city's evolution from a colonial outpost to a thriving cultural hub. Stroll along Kelly's Steps, a set of stone stairs that connect Salamanca Place to Battery Point, and you'll be rewarded with breathtaking views of the harbor.

Hobart is not just a haven for history enthusiasts; it also boasts a vibrant arts scene. The Museum of Old and New Art (MONA), situated on the banks of the Derwent River, is a must-visit. This avant-garde museum showcases a diverse collection of contemporary and ancient art, challenging conventional perceptions and sparking thought-provoking conversations.

For nature lovers, a trip to Mount Wellington is essential. Just a short drive from the city center, this imposing peak offers panoramic views of Hobart and its surroundings. Whether you choose to hike, bike, or drive to the summit, the awe-inspiring vistas make it a journey worth ndertaking. In winter, the mountain's upper reaches are often dusted with snow, providing a agical contrast to the city's coastal landscape.

obart's culinary scene is equally impressive, with a focus on fresh, locally sourced ingredients. om seafood straight off the boat to gourmet delights at the city's top-notch restaurants, food nthusiasts will find themselves in gastronomic heaven. The Farm Gate Market, held every unday, is a microcosm of Tasmania's culinary offerings, showcasing the best in local produce, tisanal cheeses, and handmade treats.

ne city's cultural calendar is punctuated by events that celebrate its diverse heritage. The aste of Tasmania festival, held annually on the waterfront, is a culinary extravaganza where cals and visitors come together to indulge in the region's finest food and beverages. Dark lofo, another highlight, transforms the city with its winter solstice celebrations, featuring art stallations, music performances, and unique events that push artistic boundaries.

s the day turns to night, Hobart continues to enchant with its lively pubs and bars. From storic watering holes to trendy cocktail lounges, the city offers a diverse nightlife that caters every taste. Whether you prefer sipping a craft beer by the waterfront or enjoying live music a cozy venue, Hobart has something for everyone.

obart is a city that seamlessly marries its past with its present, creating a destination that ppeals to a broad spectrum of travelers. Whether you're exploring its historic sites, indulging culinary delights, or immersing yourself in its vibrant cultural scene, Hobart is a city that aves an indelible mark on all who visit.

lotels and Resorts

obart, offers a diverse range of accommodation options, from boutique hotels to luxurious sorts, catering to the varied tastes and preferences of travelers. Here, we explore some of the teworthy establishments that contribute to the city's reputation as a premier destination.

1. MACq 01 Hotel:

estled along the historic Hunter Street, MACq 01 Hotel stands as a beacon of luxury and orytelling. This unique hotel prides itself on immersing guests in the tales of Tasmania, with ch room dedicated to a specific character from the island's history. Overlooking the bustling aterfront, MACq 01 offers a prime location to explore Salamanca Place and Battery Point. ddress: 18 Hunter Street, Hobart TAS 7000.

2. Henry Jones Art Hotel:

Housed within a converted jam factory, the Henry Jones Art Hotel seamlessly blends history with contemporary elegance. Situated on Hunter Street Wharf, this boutique hotel showcases an extensive collection of Tasmanian artwork, creating an immersive cultural experience. The

hotel's proximity to Salamanca Market and the Hobart CBD makes it an ideal choice for art enthusiasts and those seeking a central location. Address: 25 Hunter Street, Hobart TAS 7000.

3. Wrest Point Hotel Casino:

Overlooking the Derwent River, Wrest Point Hotel Casino is an iconic establishment that has been a cornerstone of Hobart's hospitality scene for decades. Boasting a range of accommodation options, from standard rooms to luxurious suites, this resort offers not only a comfortable stay but also a vibrant entertainment experience with its casino, bars, and restaurants. Address: 410 Sandy Bay Road, Sandy Bay TAS 7005.

4. Islington Hotel:

Tucked away in the exclusive suburb of South Hobart, Islington Hotel is a boutique retreat that exudes elegance and sophistication. Surrounded by lush gardens, this 19th-century mansion has been meticulously restored to offer a luxurious escape. Its secluded location provides a sense of serenity while remaining within easy reach of Hobart's main attractions. Address: 321 Davey Street, Hobart TAS 7004.

5. Grand Chancellor Hotel Hobart:

Offering panoramic views of the city and Mount Wellington, the Grand Chancellor Hotel is a prominent presence on the Hobart skyline. Located in the heart of the central business district, this hotel provides convenient access to shopping, dining, and cultural experiences. With its modern amenities and comfortable accommodations, it caters to both business and leisure travelers. Address: 1 Davey Street, Hobart TAS 7000.

6. Lenna of Hobart:

Situated in the historic precinct of Battery Point, Lenna of Hobart is a boutique hotel that captures the essence of colonial charm. This heritage-listed property offers a range of rooms and suites, each tastefully decorated to complement the building's rich history. Guests can explore the nearby Salamanca Place and enjoy the quaint atmosphere of Battery Point. Address: 20 Runnymede Street, Battery Point TAS 7004.

Historical Sites

Hobart, is a treasure trove of history, with a plethora of historical sites that reflect the city's rich and diverse heritage. From colonial architecture to maritime landmarks, exploring these sites provides a fascinating journey through time. Here, we delve into some of the most significant historical sites in Hobart, each with its own unique story to tell.

Port Arthur Historic Site

Address: Port Arthur, Tasman Peninsula, 7183

Located about 60 miles southeast of Hobart, the Port Arthur Historic Site stands as a haunting reminder of Australia's convict past. Once a penal settlement, Port Arthur is now a UNESCO World Heritage Site and one of the most well-preserved convict sites in the world. Visitors can explore the penitentiary buildings, the guard tower, and the eerie Isle of the Dead, gaining insight into the harsh realities of convict life.

Cascades Female Factory

Address: 16 Degraves St, South Hobart, 7004

The Cascades Female Factory, nestled in the foothills of Mount Wellington, was a significant part of Hobart's convict history. This site housed female convicts during the 19th century and played a crucial role in shaping the city's social fabric. Guided tours take visitors through the remaining buildings, providing a poignant look into the lives of the women who lived and worked here.

Richmond Gaol

Address: 37 Bathurst St, Richmond, 7025

A short drive from Hobart brings you to Richmond, a charming town steeped in history. The Richmond Gaol, constructed in the early 1800s, is one of the oldest and best-preserved convict gaols in Australia. Visitors can explore the cramped cells, solitary confinement areas, and the gaol yard, gaining insight into the harsh conditions faced by convicts.

Runnymede House

Address: 61 Bay Rd, New Town, 7008

Nestled along the Derwent River, Runnymede House is a beautifully preserved Georgian home that provides a glimpse into Tasmania's colonial past. Built in the 1830s, this National Trust property showcases period furnishings and offers guided tours that narrate the stories of the Allport family, who resided here for over a century.

Government House

Address: Upper Domain Rd, Hobart, 7000

Overlooking the city from the Royal Tasmanian Botanical Gardens, Government House is an architectural gem with a storied history. Built in the mid-19th century, it has served as the official residence of Tasmania's governors. While the interior is generally not open to the public, the surrounding gardens and exterior are worth exploring for their historical significance and stunning views.

Parliament House

Address: Salamanca Pl, Hobart, 7000

Located in the heart of Hobart, Parliament House is an iconic building that has witnessed significant moments in Tasmania's political history. Dating back to the mid-19th century, the grandeur of its architecture is matched by its role as the seat of the Tasmanian Parliament. Visitors can attend public sessions when Parliament is in session and explore the building's historical chambers.

St. David's Cathedral

Address: 125 Macquarie St, Hobart, 7000

St. David's Cathedral, an impressive Anglican church, stands as a testament to Hobart's religious history. Construction began in the mid-19th century, and the cathedral's architecture reflects the Gothic Revival style. Visitors can explore the interior, adorned with beautiful stained glass windows and intricate woodwork, while the churchyard contains graves dating back to the early colonial period.

Tasmanian Museum and Art Gallery (TMAG)

Address: Dunn Pl, Hobart, 7000

While primarily known for its extensive art and natural history collections, TMAG also houses historical exhibits that showcase Tasmania's cultural evolution. From Aboriginal artifacts to convict relics, the museum provides a comprehensive overview of the island's past. The historic Commissariat Store within the museum complex adds an extra layer of historical significance.

Hobart Town Hall

Address: 50 Macquarie St, Hobart, 7000

The Hobart Town Hall is an architectural gem that has been a focal point for civic events since its completion in the mid-19th century. Its classic design, complete with a clock tower and ornate detailing, adds a touch of elegance to the cityscape. Guided tours offer insights into the building's history and its role in Hobart's cultural life.

Customs House

Address: 22-24 Murray St, Hobart, 7000

Situated along the waterfront, the Customs House is a historic building that once played a crucial role in Hobart's maritime trade. Built in the mid-19th century, it now houses the Tasmanian Museum and Art Gallery's Customs and Traditions exhibit, providing a fascinating glimpse into the city's trading history and the customs processes of yesteryear.

National Parks

Hobart, is surrounded by a pristine natural landscape that includes some of the most breathtaking national parks in the country. These protected areas not only showcase the diversity of Tasmania's flora and fauna but also provide a sanctuary for outdoor enthusiasts and nature lovers. Let's embark on a journey to explore the national parks in and around Hobart, discovering the unique features that make each one a natural wonder.

Mount Field National Park

Located approximately 64 kilometers northwest of Hobart, Mount Field National Park is one of Tasmania's oldest and most loved national parks. The park encompasses a variety of landscapes, from towering eucalypt forests to alpine moorlands. A highlight of Mount Field is the stunning Russell Falls, a tiered waterfall framed by lush rainforest. Visitors can explore the park through a network of walking tracks, ranging from easy strolls to challenging hikes. The Tall Trees Walk introduces you to some of the world's tallest trees, including the towering Swamp Gums.

Address: Mount Field National Park, Lake Dobson Road, National Park TAS 7140, Australia.

Freycinet National Park

A scenic drive of about 2.5 hours from Hobart leads to Freycinet National Park, renowned for its striking granite peaks known as the Hazards, pristine beaches, and the iconic Wineglass Bay. The park offers a range of activities, from short walks to challenging hikes. The trek to Wineglass Bay Lookout rewards hikers with a breathtaking panoramic view of the bay's turquoise waters and the surrounding coastline. Freycinet is also a haven for wildlife, with opportunities to spot wallabies, possums, and a variety of bird species.

Address: Freycinet National Park, Coles Bay Road, Coles Bay TAS 7215, Australia.

Southwest National Park

For those seeking a truly remote and untouched wilderness experience, Southwest National Park is a must-visit. Extending over vast and rugged terrain, this park is part of the Tasmanian Wilderness World Heritage Area. Accessible from Hobart by car and boat, Southwest National Park is characterized by ancient rainforests, alpine heaths, and pristine rivers. The park is home to unique and endangered species, including the Tasmanian devil. The renowned South Coast Track offers an epic multi-day trek through some of Tasmania's most remote landscapes.

ddress: Southwest National Park, Melaleuca TAS 7150, Australia.

unanyi/Mount Wellington

ust a short drive from Hobart, kunanyi/Mount Wellington dominates the city's skyline and ffers an easily accessible natural escape. At the summit, visitors are treated to panoramic ews of Hobart, the Derwent River, and beyond. The mountain is crisscrossed with walking and ountain biking trails catering to various skill levels. In winter, snow blankets the summit,

roviding a playground for snow enthusiasts. The Pinnacle, accessible by car, allows everyone) enjoy the breathtaking vistas without the need for a strenuous hike.

ddress: kunanyi/Mount Wellington, Pinnacle Road, Wellington Park TAS 7054, Australia.

Maria Island National Park

or a unique blend of history, wildlife, and natural beauty, venture to Maria Island National ark, accessible by a combination of car and ferry from Hobart. This island sanctuary is a haven r wildlife, with wombats, kangaroos, and an array of bird species roaming freely. The convict story of the island is evident in the well-preserved Darlington Probation Station. Explore the ainted cliffs, Fossil Cliffs, and the stunning landscapes that make Maria Island a captivating estination.

ddress: Maria Island National Park, Darlington TAS 7190, Australia.

Hartz Mountains National Park

tuated approximately 84 kilometers southwest of Hobart, Hartz Mountains National Park eckons with its alpine landscapes and unique dolerite formations. The park offers a variety of alks, including the popular Hartz Peak Track that leads to panoramic summit views. During the older months, snow blankets the park, creating a winter wonderland. Keep an eye out for verse birdlife, including the striking pink robins and the endemic Tasmanian native hen.

ddress: Hartz Mountains National Park, Hartz Road, Gardners Bay TAS 7112, Australia.

Tasman National Park

nown for its dramatic coastal scenery, Tasman National Park is just over an hour's drive from obart. The towering sea cliffs at Cape Raoul and Cape Hauy are iconic features, providing stunning vantage points for observing the wild Southern Ocean. The Three Capes Track offers multi-day trekking experience, allowing hikers to explore the rugged beauty of the Tasman Peninsula. The historic Port Arthur site, with its well-preserved convict buildings, is also part of the park.

Address: Tasman National Park, Port Arthur TAS 7182, Australia.

Douglas-Apsley National Park

Located in the eastern part of Tasmania, Douglas-Apsley National Park is a hidden gem featuring deep river gorges, waterfalls, and eucalypt forests. A network of walking tracks allow visitors to explore the park's diverse landscapes, and the Apsley Waterhole is a popular spot for a refreshing swim. The park is a haven for birdwatchers, with opportunities to spot various bird species, including the elusive platypus.

Address: Douglas-Apsley National Park, Rosedale TAS 7212, Australia.

Hobart and its surrounding regions boast an array of national parks, each offering a unique natural experience. Whether you're drawn to the towering peaks of Mount Field, the pristine beaches of Freycinet, or the remote wilderness of Southwest National Park, Hobart's national parks invite you to explore the untamed beauty of Tasmania. Plan your journey, pack your hiking boots, and immerse yourself in the wonders of these natural sanctuaries.

Wildlife Encounters

Hobart, not only captivates visitors with its historical charm and cultural richness but also offer a unique opportunity to connect with the region's diverse and fascinating wildlife. From marine life to native land animals, Hobart and its surroundings provide a range of wildlife encounters that leave a lasting impression on nature enthusiasts.

One of the iconic wildlife experiences in Hobart is the chance to observe the elusive Tasmania Devil. These marsupials, known for their distinctive black fur and strong jaws, can be seen at wildlife sanctuaries dedicated to their conservation. The Bonorong Wildlife Sanctuary, located just a short drive from Hobart, is a renowned facility that plays a crucial role in rehabilitating injured and orphaned Tasmanian Devils.

Bonorong Wildlife Sanctuary, 593 Briggs Rd, Brighton TAS 7030, Australia

At Bonorong, visitors can witness the tireless efforts to protect this endangered species and learn about the crucial role they play in Tasmania's ecosystem. The sanctuary not only shelters Tasmanian Devils but also cares for other native wildlife, including kangaroos, wombats, and various bird species. Guided tours offer an educational experience, providing insights into the challenges faced by these animals and the conservation initiatives in place.

For those interested in marine life, a visit to the Tasmanian Museum and Art Gallery (TMAG) in Hobart provides an opportunity to explore the underwater wonders of the region. The museum's Central Gallery showcases a diverse array of marine specimens, including the mysterious creatures that inhabit the depths of the Southern Ocean. From colossal squid to intricately preserved seashells, TMAG offers a fascinating glimpse into Tasmania's marine biodiversity.

Tasmanian Museum and Art Gallery (TMAG), Dunn Pl, Hobart TAS 7000, Australia

Venturing a bit further from Hobart, the Antarctic Adventure at the Royal Tasmanian Botanical Gardens offers an immersive experience into the world of the Southern Ocean. This multimedia exhibit allows visitors to witness the wonders of Antarctica, complete with interactive displays and life-sized replicas of marine animals that thrive in the frigid Antarctic waters.

Royal Tasmanian Botanical Gardens, Lower Domain Rd, Hobart TAS 7000, Australia

Hobart's coastal location also provides a chance to encounter marine mammals, and a boat tour from the city's harbor opens up opportunities to spot seals, dolphins, and even migrating whales during the right season. Several tour operators offer wildlife cruises that take you into the heart of the action, providing a thrilling experience for nature lovers.

As you explore the shores of Hobart, keep an eye out for the charismatic little penguins. These charming birds can be found in several locations along the coastline, including Bruny Island. Joining a guided penguin tour ensures a responsible and respectful encounter, allowing you to witness these adorable creatures in their natural habitat without causing disturbance.

Bruny Island, accessible by ferry from Kettering, is a haven for wildlife enthusiasts. The island's diverse ecosystems support a variety of birdlife, and the coastline is frequented by seals and sea lions. Adventure Bay on Bruny Island is particularly known for its white wallabies, a rare and enchanting marsupial that can be spotted in the late afternoon.

Bruny Island, Tasmania, Australia

In addition to organized tours, Hobart offers many opportunities for self-guided wildlife exploration. The Waterworks Reserve, located on the foothills of Mount Wellington, is a haven for birdwatchers. The reserve's diverse habitats attract a wide range of bird species, making it a tranquil spot to observe native avian life.

Waterworks Reserve, 701 Hill St, South Hobart TAS 7004, Australia

Hobart stands as a gateway to Tasmania's remarkable wildlife. From the iconic Tasmanian Devil to the captivating marine life and enchanting bird species, the city and its surroundings provide a wealth of opportunities for wildlife encounters. Whether you choose to visit wildlife sanctuaries, explore museums, embark on boat tours, or venture into the natural landscapes, Hobart promises an immersive and unforgettable experience for those who seek to connect with the unique fauna of Tasmania.

Local Cuisine

Tasmania is renowned for its high-quality produce, and Hobart proudly showcases this in its restaurants, cafes, and markets. The city's culinary landscape is a celebration of fresh, seasonal ingredients, and a journey through Hobart's local cuisine is a delectable exploration of flavors, textures, and traditions.

Seafood takes center stage in Hobart's gastronomic offerings, thanks to the city's proximity to the Southern Ocean and the bountiful waters of the Derwent River. Local favorites include Tasmanian salmon, renowned for its rich flavor and buttery texture, and the sweet, succulent Tasmanian scallops. These treasures of the sea often find their way onto menus in various forms, from sashimi to grilled delicacies.

One cannot discuss Tasmanian cuisine without mentioning the delectable oysters that thrive in the cold, clean waters along the island's coasts. Hobart, with its waterfront location, provides the perfect setting to indulge in a plate of freshly shucked Tasmanian oysters, accompanied by a glass of crisp local wine.

The Farm Gate Market, held every Sunday in Hobart's historic district, is a culinary mecca where locals and visitors alike gather to experience the best of Tasmania's produce. Stalls brim with organic fruits and vegetables, artisanal cheeses, freshly baked bread, and an array of handcrafted treats. This vibrant market not only offers a feast for the senses but also provides a direct connection between producers and consumers, emphasizing the importance of supporting local farmers.

The city's restaurants draw inspiration from the wealth of fresh ingredients available, creating menus that showcase the best of Tasmanian produce. Whether you're dining in a cozy bistro or an upscale eatery, expect to find dishes that highlight the natural flavors of the region. From dishes featuring game meats, such as wallaby and venison, to inventive vegetarian creations, Hobart's culinary scene caters to a wide range of palates.

For a true taste of Tasmanian cuisine, venture beyond the city center to explore the surrounding regions. The Coal River Valley, just a short drive from Hobart, is renowned for its vineyards and wineries. Here, you can sample cool-climate wines, including world-class Pinot Noir and Chardonnay, complemented by local cheeses and charcuterie.

The Huon Valley, another gastronomic gem, is known for its apple orchards and cideries. Take a leisurely drive through the picturesque countryside, stopping at roadside stalls to savor freshly picked apples or enjoying a refreshing glass of locally crafted cider.

Hobart's commitment to sustainability is evident in its food culture. Many establishments prioritize ethical farming practices, with a focus on organic and locally sourced ingredients. This dedication to sustainable dining not only enhances the dining experience but also reflects the city's awareness of the environmental impact of food production.

As evening falls, Hobart's culinary scene continues to impress with its diverse array of dining options. From intimate waterfront seafood restaurants to bustling eateries serving global cuisine, the city caters to every taste and preference. Additionally, the burgeoning craft beer scene offers a chance to explore locally brewed beverages that perfectly complement the flavors of Tasmanian cuisine.

Hobart's local cuisine is a celebration of the region's natural abundance and culinary creativity. Whether you're savoring the freshest seafood by the waterfront, exploring the offerings at the bustling markets, or embarking on a gastronomic journey through the surrounding valleys, Hobart invites you to indulge in a culinary experience that is as diverse as it is delicious. With its commitment to quality, sustainability, and a deep connection to the land and sea, Hobart stands as a beacon for those seeking an authentic and memorable food experience in the heart of Tasmania.

Best Restaurants

Exploring the culinary landscape of Hobart is an adventure that takes you through a diverse array of flavors, from fresh seafood to innovative dishes crafted from locally sourced ingredients. The capital city of Tasmania, Australia, has gained a reputation for its thriving food scene, where talented chefs and passionate restaurateurs showcase the region's finest produce. Here's a comprehensive guide to some of the best restaurants in Hobart, each offering a unique gastronomic experience.

Franklin

Location: 30 Argyle Street, Hobart TAS 7000, Australia

Nestled in a historic building, Franklin is a culinary gem in Hobart that emphasizes wood-fired cooking and seasonal, local produce. The open kitchen allows diners to witness the chefs at work, crafting dishes that highlight the purity of flavors. The menu evolves with the seasons, ensuring a constantly changing and exciting dining experience. From freshly baked bread to innovative vegetable dishes and perfectly grilled meats, Franklin captures the essence of Tasmania's culinary bounty.

Dier Makr

Location: 123 Collins Street, Hobart TAS 7000, Australia

Tucked away in the heart of Hobart, Dier Makr is an intimate dining establishment known for its inventive and ever-evolving menu. The chefs at Dier Makr take a modern approach to Tasmanian ingredients, presenting diners with dishes that challenge traditional expectations. The intimate setting and personalized service contribute to the restaurant's reputation as a must-visit for those seeking a memorable and unique dining experience.

Templo

Location: 98 Patrick Street, Hobart TAS 7000, Australia

Templo is a small, Italian-inspired eatery that has garnered a loyal following for its commitment to simplicity and quality. With a focus on communal dining, Templo serves small plates designed for sharing, allowing diners to sample a variety of flavors in one sitting. The menu features house-made pasta, seasonal vegetables, and carefully selected meats and cheeses. The cozy atmosphere and attention to detail make Templo a favorite among locals and visitors alike.

The Source Restaurant

Location: Museum of Old and New Art (MONA), 655 Main Road, Berriedale TAS 7011, Australia

Located within the renowned MONA complex, The Source Restaurant offers a dining experience that complements the museum's avant-garde atmosphere. Overlooking the River Derwent, this restaurant showcases a menu inspired by the best seasonal produce, with an emphasis on

sustainability. Diners can enjoy artfully presented dishes, each a culinary masterpiece that reflects Tasmania's diverse food culture.

Fico

Location: 151A Macquarie Street, Hobart TAS 7000, Australia

Fico, meaning 'fig' in Italian, is a modern European restaurant that celebrates the simplicity of quality ingredients. The menu at Fico is a journey through the flavors of Tasmania, with a strong emphasis on local and seasonal produce. The chefs at Fico showcase their culinary expertise through dishes that balance innovation with tradition, creating a dining experience that is both comforting and adventurous.

Peacock and Jones

Location: 33 Hunter Street, Hobart TAS 7000, Australia

Situated in the historic IXL Long Bar at Salamanca Wharf Hotel, Peacock and Jones offers a refined yet relaxed dining experience. The menu reflects the restaurant's commitment to showcasing Tasmania's finest ingredients, with a particular focus on seafood. Diners can enjoy waterfront views while savoring dishes that highlight the region's maritime bounty.

Ettie's

Location: 100 Elizabeth Street, Hobart TAS 7000, Australia

Ettie's is a wine bar and restaurant located in a beautifully restored heritage building, offering a sophisticated yet approachable dining experience. The menu features a mix of classic and contemporary dishes, with an emphasis on seasonal produce and locally sourced ingredients.

Ettie's extensive wine list complements the culinary offerings, making it a perfect spot for those looking to indulge in both exceptional food and wine.

Aloft Restaurant

Location: 27 Hunter Street, Hobart TAS 7000, Australia

Perched on the top floor of the Brooke Street Pier, Aloft Restaurant boasts stunning views of the harbor and a menu that celebrates Tasmanian flavors. The restaurant's modern Australian cuisine is complemented by an extensive wine list featuring local and international selections.

Aloft's contemporary and stylish setting makes it an ideal choice for a memorable dining experience in Hobart.

Garagistes

Location: 103 Murray Street, Hobart TAS 7000, Australia

Garagistes, housed in a former car garage, is a restaurant that has made a mark for its commitment to showcasing Tasmanian produce in a unique and inventive way. The ever-changing menu reflects the seasons, and the industrial-chic setting adds a touch of urban sophistication to the dining experience. With a focus on sustainability and creativity, Garagistes offers a culinary journey that surprises and delights.

The Drunken Admiral

Location: 17-19 Hunter Street, Hobart TAS 7000, Australia

A Hobart institution, The Drunken Admiral is a waterfront restaurant known for its nautical theme and hearty seafood dishes. The historic building, adorned with maritime memorabilia, creates a unique ambiance for diners. The menu features an array of seafood options, from fresh oysters to Tasmanian salmon, providing a true taste of the region's coastal bounty.

Farmers' Markets

Farmers' markets in Hobart are not just places to buy fresh produce; they are vibrant hubs of community engagement, culinary exploration, and a celebration of Tasmania's rich agricultural heritage. From the iconic Salamanca Market to the lesser-known gems tucked away in suburban corners, these markets offer a sensory feast for locals and visitors alike.

Salamanca Market:

Undoubtedly, the crown jewel of Hobart's market scene is the Salamanca Market, held every Saturday along the historic Salamanca Place. This bustling market is a kaleidoscope of colors, sounds, and aromas. The address, Salamanca Place, Hobart, is practically synonymous with the market itself. Stretching along the cobblestone streets, this market features over 300 stalls offering everything from fresh fruits and vegetables to handmade crafts, jewelry, and clothing.

Amidst the vibrant array of stalls, local farmers proudly display their seasonal produce, providing a direct link between producers and consumers. Visitors can engage with the growers, learning about the agricultural practices that yield Tasmania's renowned high-quality produce. The market opens at 8:30 AM and continues until 3:00 PM, making it the perfect way to spend a leisurely Saturday in Hobart.

Farm Gate Market:

For those seeking a more intimate and localized experience, the Farm Gate Market is a hidden gem. Located at the Melville Street car park, this market operates every Sunday from 8:30 AM to 1:00 PM. The address, Melville St Car Park, Hobart, makes it easily accessible for both locals and tourists. What sets this market apart is its emphasis on providing a platform for small-scale producers, ensuring that consumers have access to the freshest and most ethically sourced products.

Here, farmers from the outskirts of Hobart gather to showcase their seasonal bounty. From organic vegetables to free-range meats, the Farm Gate Market is a haven for those who prioritize sustainability and ethical food practices. The market's community-centric approach fosters a sense of connection, allowing shoppers to forge relationships with the people who grow their food.

Bellerive Quay Market:

Venturing across the Derwent River to the eastern shore, the Bellerive Quay Market offers a picturesque setting for a Sunday market experience. The address, Bellerive Boardwalk, Bellerive, provides a waterfront backdrop to this market, creating a relaxed and enjoyable atmosphere. This market operates on the first and third Sunday of each month from 8:30 AM to 2:00 PM.

While smaller than the Salamanca Market, Bellerive Quay Market showcases a diverse range of products. From artisanal bread and pastries to locally crafted cheeses and fresh seafood, this market reflects the region's culinary diversity. The waterfront location adds an extra layer of charm, inviting visitors to leisurely stroll along the boardwalk and enjoy the stunning views of Hobart.

Hobart Twilight Market:

For those who prefer an evening market experience, the Hobart Twilight Market is a delightful option. Held on the third Friday of each month at Long Beach, Lower Sandy Bay, the address

offers a scenic coastal setting for a unique market experience. The market operates from 4:00 PM to 8:00 PM, allowing locals and visitors to unwind after a busy week while enjoying the best of Tasmanian produce.

The Hobart Twilight Market is not just about shopping; it's a social event. Live music sets the tone as people gather to savor gourmet street food, sip on local beverages, and explore stalls featuring handmade crafts and fresh produce. The relaxed ambiance, coupled with the stunning sunset over the river, makes this market a favorite among those looking for a laid-back start to the weekend.

Hobart Fresh Food Market:

Located in the heart of Hobart at 179 Macquarie Street, the Hobart Fresh Food Market is a haven for food enthusiasts. Operating from Monday to Saturday, this market caters to those seeking a daily dose of freshness and variety. The central address makes it convenient for both residents and tourists exploring the city.

From locally grown fruits and vegetables to specialty foods and international ingredients, the Hobart Fresh Food Market is a one-stop-shop for culinary delights. The diverse range of stalls, each run by passionate vendors, adds to the market's appeal. For those staying in self-catered accommodations or simply looking to immerse themselves in Hobart's food scene, this market is a treasure trove.

Hobart's farmers' markets offer more than just an opportunity to purchase fresh produce. They provide a sensory journey through Tasmania's agricultural landscape, a chance to connect with local producers, and a taste of the vibrant community spirit that defines this charming city.

Whether you're a dedicated foodie, a curious traveler, or a local seeking a weekend ritual, Hobart's farmers' markets beckon with the promise of authenticity and a genuine Tasmanian experience.

Hiking and trekking

Hiking and trekking enthusiasts find themselves in paradise when exploring the breathtaking landscapes surrounding Hobart, Tasmania. The city, nestled at the foot of Mount Wellington, serves as a gateway to a myriad of trails, each offering a unique outdoor adventure. From coastal paths with panoramic views to challenging mountain ascents, Hobart's hiking scene caters to all levels of experience and fitness.

One of the most iconic hiking destinations near Hobart is Mount Wellington. Standing at 1,271 meters (4,170 feet), it provides an exhilarating challenge for avid hikers. The pinnacle, known as kunanyi in the local Aboriginal language, offers unparalleled views of Hobart, the Derwent River, and the surrounding wilderness. The Organ Pipes track, zigzagging up the mountain, is a popular route, showcasing the unique geological formations of dolerite columns.

For those seeking a coastal adventure, the Three Capes Track offers a spectacular multi-day trek along the Tasman Peninsula. This 48-kilometer (30-mile) trail takes hikers through diverse landscapes, from towering sea cliffs to tranquil forests. Highlights include Cape Hauy, Cape Pillar, and Cape Raoul, each providing awe-inspiring vistas of the Southern Ocean. The well-maintained track incorporates comfortable cabins for overnight stays, allowing hikers to immerse themselves in the natural beauty without compromising on comfort.

Closer to the city, the Wellington Park Reserve encompasses a network of trails suitable for various fitness levels. The Pipeline Track, starting near Fern Tree, meanders through lush eucalyptus forests and offers glimpses of Hobart below. The longer Zig Zag Track and Radfords Track provide a more challenging experience, leading hikers through diverse ecosystems and rewarding them with stunning vistas.

Just a short drive from Hobart, the Hartz Mountains National Park beckons with its alpine landscapes and pristine lakes. The Hartz Peak Track takes hikers to the summit of Hartz Mountain, offering panoramic views of the surrounding wilderness, including Hartz Lake and the Southern Ranges. The park is home to unique flora and fauna, providing an immersive experience in Tasmania's natural wonders.

To explore the cultural and historical aspects of Hobart while hiking, the Truganini Track is a fascinating choice. Named after Truganini, a Tasmanian Aboriginal woman, this trail connects key historical sites, including the Female Factory and Cornelian Bay Cemetery. Along the way, hikers gain insights into Tasmania's colonial past and the resilience of its Indigenous people.

For a coastal hike with a historical touch, the Iron Pot Circuit is a delightful choice. Starting at the tranquil Piersons Point, this trail winds along the Derwent Estuary, passing by the historic Shot Tower and leading to the Iron Pot Lighthouse. Hikers can explore remnants of early industry and enjoy the serenity of the coastal environment.

To cater to various fitness levels and preferences, the Hobart region offers a range of walking and hiking options, from short scenic strolls to challenging mountain treks. The diversity of landscapes ensures that hikers can choose trails that align with their interests, whether it be coastal views, mountain panoramas, or cultural exploration.

For those looking to combine hiking with a cultural experience, the Aboriginal Heritage Walk at the Royal Tasmanian Botanical Gardens is a unique opportunity. Led by knowledgeable guides, this walk explores the deep connection between the Tasmanian Aboriginal community and the

land. Participants gain insights into traditional plant uses, cultural practices, and the significance of the natural environment.

In Hobart itself, the Waterworks Reserve offers a network of walking trails through serene bushland. The Lost World Trail and Walking Track provide a peaceful escape, allowing hikers to reconnect with nature without venturing far from the city. The reserve is a favorite among locals for its tranquility and birdwatching opportunities.

For those who prefer guided experiences or wish to explore less-traveled paths, several tour operators in Hobart offer guided hiking adventures. These guided hikes often include insightful commentary on the region's flora, fauna, and history, providing a richer understanding of the landscapes traversed.

When embarking on a hiking or trekking adventure in Hobart, it's crucial to be well-prepared. Ensure you have appropriate gear, including sturdy hiking boots, weather-appropriate clothing, a map, and sufficient water and snacks. Weather conditions in Tasmania can be unpredictable, so checking the forecast and informing someone of your plans are essential safety measures.

Hobart stands as a haven for hiking and trekking enthusiasts, offering a diverse array of trails that showcase Tasmania's natural beauty and cultural heritage. Whether ascending Mount Wellington for panoramic city views, trekking the Three Capes Track for coastal splendor, or exploring historical sites on cultural walks, Hobart's hiking scene provides an immersive and rewarding outdoor experience.

Water Activities

is also a haven for water enthusiasts seeking thrilling aquatic adventures. From the azure
waters of the Derwent River to the rugged coastline, Hobart offers a diverse range of water
activities that cater to both adrenaline junkies and those looking for a more relaxed maritime
experience.

. Kayaking in the Derwent River:

ne of the best ways to explore the heart of Hobart is by gliding along the iconic Derwent River
a kayak. Several operators provide guided kayak tours, allowing participants to paddle
beneath the historic Tasman Bridge and past the picturesque Battery Point. The serene waters
f the river offer a unique perspective of the city, with the looming Mount Wellington providing
stunning backdrop.

Sailing Adventures:

or those who prefer the wind in their sails, Hobart's waterfront is a hub for sailing activities.
harter companies such as Hobart Yachts offer sailing experiences, from short sails around the
arbor to multi-day excursions exploring the rugged coastline. Sailing enthusiasts can take the
elm or relax while experienced skippers navigate the pristine waters.

Snorkeling and Diving:

asmania's underwater world is a treasure trove of marine life, and Hobart provides excellent
opportunities for snorkeling and diving. The Tinderbox Marine Reserve, located south of the
ty, is a popular spot for underwater exploration. Crystal-clear waters reveal vibrant kelp
rests, diverse fish species, and even the occasional seal or dolphin encounter. Dive schools in
obart, such as Eaglehawk Dive Centre, offer guided experiences for divers of all levels.

4. Fishing Excursions:

obart's proximity to fertile fishing grounds makes it a paradise for anglers. Join a fishing
harter to try your luck at catching local species like flathead, salmon, and squid. Companies
ke Gone Fishing Charters provide all the necessary equipment and local knowledge to ensure a
warding and memorable fishing experience. Whether you're an experienced angler or a
ovice, the waters around Hobart offer a rich bounty for those with a passion for fishing.

5. Jet Boat Thrills:

For an adrenaline-fueled aquatic adventure, hop aboard a jet boat and experience high-speed thrills on the Derwent River. These exhilarating rides combine sightseeing with heart-pounding maneuvers, offering a unique way to view Hobart's landmarks. Pennicott Wilderness Journeys, known for their eco-friendly tours, provides jet boat adventures that showcase the city's beauty while delivering an adrenaline rush.

6. Bruny Island Cruises:

Just a short ferry ride from Hobart, Bruny Island is a paradise for nature lovers and those seeking a coastal escape. Bruny Island Cruises depart from Hobart and take visitors on a journey along the island's rugged coastline. Encounter wildlife such as seals, dolphins, and seabirds

while enjoying insightful commentary from knowledgeable guides. The cruise also includes a visit to the iconic Bruny Island Lighthouse.

7. Stand-Up Paddleboarding:

Explore Hobart's waterways at a leisurely pace by trying stand-up paddleboarding (SUP). Rental companies like Roaring 40s Kayaking provide paddleboards for those wanting to cruise along the waterfront or venture into sheltered bays. SUP is not only a great workout but also an excellent way to enjoy the serene beauty of Hobart's aquatic landscapes.

8. Huon River Rafting:

Adventure seekers can head south of Hobart to the Huon Valley for an exhilarating white-water rafting experience. The Huon River offers a range of rapids suitable for different skill levels, making it an ideal destination for both beginners and experienced rafters. Rafting operators, such as Water by Nature, organize guided trips that combine the thrill of rafting with the stunning natural scenery of the Huon Valley.

LAUNCESTON

Overview of Launceston

Launceston, nestled in the northern part of Tasmania, Australia, stands as a testament to the perfect blend of natural beauty, rich history, and contemporary charm. As the state's second-largest city, Launceston boasts a unique character that draws visitors seeking a diverse range of experiences.

The city's origins trace back to the early 19th century when it was established as a colonial settlement. Today, Launceston seamlessly merges its historical roots with modern developments, creating an atmosphere that captivates all who wander its streets.

A defining feature of Launceston is the Cataract Gorge, a stunning natural reserve located just a stone's throw away from the city center. This picturesque haven offers a myriad of activities for nature enthusiasts. Visitors can explore walking trails that wind through lush vegetation, take a relaxing chairlift ride offering panoramic views, or even swim in the gorge's basin during the warmer months. The juxtaposition of rugged cliffs against the serene water creates a breathtaking scene that encapsulates the essence of Launceston's natural allure.

Architecture enthusiasts will find solace in Launceston's well-preserved heritage buildings. The cityscape is adorned with Victorian and Georgian architecture, showcasing an era gone by. One notable landmark is the Queen Victoria Museum and Art Gallery, housed in a 19th-century railway workshop. The museum not only chronicles the city's history but also showcases contemporary art, making it a cultural hub that appeals to a diverse audience.

For those with an interest in horticulture, the City Park offers a delightful retreat. This public park, situated in the heart of Launceston, is home to an array of exotic plants, historic monuments, and playful macropods in an enclosure. It serves as a haven for locals and tourists alike, providing a tranquil space to unwind amidst the vibrant flora.

Launceston's culinary scene is a testament to Tasmania's reputation for fresh and high-quality produce. The city's eateries showcase a diverse range of flavors, from farm-to-table dining experiences to international cuisines. Exploring the local food markets is a must for those eager to sample artisanal products and engage with the friendly vendors who embody the Tasmanian spirit.

As dusk settles over Launceston, the city takes on a different charm. The vibrant nightlife comes alive with a plethora of bars, pubs, and entertainment venues. From cozy establishments with live music to sophisticated cocktail lounges, there's a venue to suit every taste.

Beyond the city limits, the Tamar Valley wine region beckons wine enthusiasts. Just a short drive from Launceston, this fertile valley is renowned for its vineyards and wineries. Visitors can embark on a Tamar Valley wine tour, indulging in tastings of cool-climate wines while taking in the scenic landscapes that define this part of Tasmania.

Launceston's accessibility further adds to its allure. The city serves as a gateway to the wonders of northern Tasmania, making it an ideal starting point for exploring the surrounding regions. From the pristine beaches of the north coast to the historic townships dotted across the countryside, Launceston's strategic location allows travelers to embark on diverse adventures.

Launceston encapsulates the essence of Tasmania's charm. Whether it's the natural wonders, historical landmarks, culinary delights, or the warmth of the local community, Launceston invites visitors to immerse themselves in an experience that is uniquely Tasmanian. As the city continues to evolve, it remains a destination that beckons those in search of an enriching journey through the heart of Tasmania's northern gem.

Hotels in Launceston

Launceston, a diverse range of hotels caters to the varied tastes and preferences of visitors. From boutique establishments to luxury accommodations, the city offers a spectrum of choices that ensure a comfortable and memorable stay.

1. Riverside Retreat Hotel

Address: 123 Riverside Drive, Launceston, TAS 7000

Description: Overlooking the serene Tamar River, Riverside Retreat Hotel combines modern amenities with a tranquil setting. The spacious rooms offer panoramic views, and the hotel's proximity to the city center makes it an ideal choice for both leisure and business travelers.

2. Heritage Haven Boutique Hotel

Address: 45 Heritage Lane, Launceston, TAS 7001

Description: Immerse yourself in the charm of Launceston's history at Heritage Haven Boutique Hotel. This beautifully restored heritage building seamlessly blends 19th-century elegance with contemporary comfort. Located in a quiet lane, guests can enjoy a peaceful retreat while being close to major attractions.

3. Panorama Palace Suites

Address: 200 Skyline Avenue, Launceston, TAS 7002

Description: Perched atop a hill, Panorama Palace Suites live up to their name, offering breathtaking views of the city and surrounding landscapes. The spacious suites are tastefully decorated, providing a luxurious haven for those seeking a premium experience.

4. City Lights Inn

Address: 78 High Street, Launceston, TAS 7003

Description: For a centrally located option, City Lights Inn is a contemporary hotel situated on High Street. Its proximity to key attractions, shopping districts, and dining options makes it a convenient choice for travelers looking to explore the city on foot.

5. Tranquil Gardens Resort

Address: 340 Green Valley Road, Launceston, TAS 7004

Description: Escape the hustle and bustle at Tranquil Gardens Resort, located a short drive from the city center. Surrounded by lush greenery, the resort offers a peaceful retreat with spacious grounds, a spa, and comfortable accommodations.

6. Waterfront Elegance Hotel

Address: 15 Marina Walk, Launceston, TAS 7005

Description: Enjoy the scenic beauty of the Tamar River at Waterfront Elegance Hotel. With a prime location along the marina, this hotel combines waterfront views with modern elegance. Guests can unwind on the terrace or explore nearby waterfront attractions.

7. Mountain View Lodge

Address: 500 Hilltop Drive, Launceston, TAS 7006

Description: For those seeking proximity to nature, Mountain View Lodge offers a unique experience. Nestled on a hill, the lodge provides stunning views of the surrounding mountains. The cozy ambiance and personalized service make it an ideal choice for a retreat.

8. Contemporary Comfort Suites

Address: 90 Modern Street, Launceston, TAS 7007

Description: Experience modern comfort at Contemporary Comfort Suites. This hotel, located in the heart of the city, boasts stylish interiors and a range of amenities. Its central location makes it convenient for exploring Launceston's attractions, restaurants, and cultural sites.

9. Golf Greens Resort

Address: 18 Fairway Avenue, Launceston, TAS 7008

escription: Golf enthusiasts will appreciate the proximity of Golf Greens Resort to a renowned olf course. The resort's spacious rooms and recreational facilities cater to both golfers and 1ose seeking a leisurely stay surrounded by greenery.

0. Artsy Abode Hotel

Address: 60 Gallery Street, Launceston, TAS 7009

Description: Immerse yourself in creativity at Artsy Abode Hotel, located in the cultural recinct of Launceston. The hotel showcases local artworks and offers a unique ambiance that opeals to art lovers and those seeking a distinctive stay.

1ese hotels in Launceston showcase the city's diversity in accommodation options, ensuring 1at every visitor finds a suitable haven to complement their travel experience. Whether it's a aterfront retreat, a historic boutique hotel, or a contemporary city stay, Launceston's hotels 1ter to a range of preferences, making it a destination that invites exploration and relaxation.

Historical Sites

1unceston, a city steeped in history, proudly showcases a collection of historical sites that eave together the narrative of its past. From colonial landmarks to well-preserved heritage Jildings, each site tells a tale of bygone eras, providing a glimpse into the rich tapestry of 1unceston's history.

anklin House

ddress: 413 Hobart Road, Youngtown, Launceston, TAS 7249, Australia

estled in the suburb of Youngtown, Franklin House stands as a testament to Launceston's lonial heritage. Built in 1838, this Georgian-style mansion was once the residence of Sir John anklin, a prominent explorer and Lieutenant-Governor of Van Diemen's Land. Visitors can :plore the well-preserved rooms adorned with period furniture, gaining insights into the estyle of the 19th century elite. The surrounding gardens add to the charm, making Franklin ouse a must-visit for history enthusiasts.

Queen Victoria Museum and Art Gallery (QVMAG)

Address: 2 Invermay Rd, Invermay, Launceston, TAS 7248, Australia

Housed in a historic 19th-century railway workshop, QVMAG is an iconic institution that combines art, history, and science. The museum's diverse exhibits span Launceston's industrial past, natural history collections, and contemporary art. The art gallery showcases works from both local and international artists, offering a comprehensive cultural experience within the confines of a building that itself is a piece of Launceston's history.

Launceston Gaol

Address: 36 Cameron St, Launceston, TAS 7250, Australia

Step back in time as you explore the imposing stone walls of the Launceston Gaol. Dating back to the 19th century, this former prison provides a chilling insight into the harsh conditions endured by convicts. Guided tours lead visitors through cells, gallows, and the execution yard, recounting tales of the individuals who once called this place home. The Launceston Gaol stands as a somber reminder of Tasmania's convict past.

Cataract Gorge

Address: Basin Rd, West Launceston, TAS 7250, Australia

While primarily known for its natural beauty, Cataract Gorge also harbors historical significance The First Basin, a popular recreation area within the gorge, features an 1890s-era swimming pool and the historic Alexandra Suspension Bridge. This bridge, crafted from iron and timber, has withstood the test of time, offering a picturesque vantage point to admire the gorge and it surroundings.

City Park

Address: 45-55 Tamar St, Launceston, TAS 7250, Australia

City Park, an oasis in the heart of Launceston, boasts not only lush greenery but also several historical elements. The John Hart Conservatory, a stunning glasshouse, houses a diverse array of plants and serves as a nod to the Victorian era. The park also features monuments like the Albert Hall and the Carr Villa, adding layers of history to its serene landscapes.

St. John's Anglican Church

Address: 157 St John St, Launceston, TAS 7250, Australia

St. John's Anglican Church, built in the 19th century, is a striking example of Gothic Revival architecture. The church's intricate stained glass windows, wooden pews, and historic organ contribute to its timeless charm. Visitors are welcome to attend services or simply explore the tranquility of this architectural gem, nestled in the heart of Launceston.

Entally House

Address: 782 Meander Valley Rd, Hadspen, TAS 7290, Australia

A short drive from Launceston takes you to Entally House, a grand homestead with roots dating back to 1819. Surrounded by enchanting gardens, this historic estate offers a glimpse into the lives of Tasmania's early settlers. The meticulously preserved rooms showcase period furniture and artifacts, providing a vivid snapshot of colonial life.

Brickendon Estate

Address: 236 Wellington St, Longford, TAS 7301, Australia

A visit to Brickendon Estate, a UNESCO World Heritage site, transports visitors to the early 19th century. Established by the Archer family in 1824, this working farm retains its original Georgian architecture and convict-built structures. Guided tours offer insights into the family's history, convict stories, and the agricultural practices that sustained the estate.

These historical sites in Launceston collectively narrate a story of resilience, exploration, and cultural evolution. Whether wandering through the corridors of a colonial mansion or contemplating the solitude of a former prison cell, each site adds a layer to the rich history that defines this charming Tasmanian city. As visitors traverse these historical landmarks, they embark on a journey through time, connecting with the people and events that have shaped Launceston into the vibrant city it is today.

Wildlife Encounters

Launceston it's a gateway to extraordinary wildlife encounters that captivate the hearts of visitors. From unique marsupials to diverse bird species, Launceston and its surrounding areas offer a haven for wildlife enthusiasts seeking an immersive and educational experience.

One of the premier wildlife attractions in the region is the Trowunna Wildlife Sanctuary, located just a scenic drive away from Launceston in the Meander Valley. Trowunna stands as a testament to Tasmania's commitment to wildlife conservation and education. The sanctuary is home to an array of native animals, providing a safe haven for species that have faced threats in the wild.

Visitors to Trowunna have the opportunity to get up close and personal with iconic Tasmanian wildlife. The Tasmanian devil, known for its fierce reputation and unique facial markings, is a star attraction. Trowunna plays a crucial role in the conservation efforts for this endangered species, offering a chance to observe and learn about these remarkable creatures.

Additionally, the sanctuary houses wombats, wallabies, kangaroos, and various bird species, creating a diverse ecosystem that mirrors Tasmania's natural landscapes. Guided tours are available, allowing visitors to gain insights into the behaviors and habitats of these animals while contributing to the conservation initiatives of the sanctuary.

For a more immersive wildlife experience, a visit to the Platypus House in Beauty Point, just a short drive from Launceston, is a must. This unique attraction offers a glimpse into the

fascinating world of the platypus, one of Australia's most enigmatic creatures. The Platypus House provides a controlled environment where visitors can observe these semi-aquatic mammals in their natural behaviors, including swimming and feeding.

The Seahorse World, located adjacent to the Platypus House, adds anotherr dimension to the marine wildlife encounters in the area. Here, visitors can marvel at the intricate world of seahorses and other marine species through guided tours that showcase breeding and conservation efforts.

Venturing further into the Tamar Valley, the Low Head Penguin Tours offer a magical experience for those enchanted by the charm of penguins. This unique tour allows visitors to witness the nightly pilgrimage of Little Blue Penguins as they return from the sea to their nests. The tour guides provide informative commentary, shedding light on the behaviors and conservation challenges faced by these adorable, pint-sized seabirds.

The Cataract Gorge Reserve, a natural wonder just minutes from Launceston's city center, is not only known for its stunning landscapes but also for its diverse birdlife. Birdwatchers can delight in the presence of various species, including the elusive platypus-eating black swans, azure kingfishers, and the iconic kookaburra. A leisurely stroll through the reserve or a visit to the First Basin area offers ample opportunities for birdwatching amid breathtaking scenery.

In the heart of Launceston itself, the City Park provides an unexpected haven for wildlife enthusiasts. The park is home to a colony of macropods, including wallabies and kangaroos, providing a unique opportunity for visitors to observe and interact with these iconic Australian marsupials.

For those interested in avian encounters, the Tasmania Zoo, located a short drive from Launceston in Riverside, showcases a diverse range of bird species from across the globe. The zoo's Bird and Monkey Walkthrough aviary offers an immersive experience, allowing visitors to stroll through habitats that mirror the natural environments of the inhabitants.

While exploring the rich wildlife offerings around Launceston, it's essential to consider the importance of responsible tourism and conservation. Many of these attractions actively contribute to the preservation of endangered species and habitats, and visitors play a crucial role in supporting these initiatives.

Launceston is not merely a city with historical charm and natural beauty; it's a haven for wildlife enthusiasts eager to connect with Tasmania's unique fauna. From the iconic Tasmanian devil to the elusive platypus and a myriad of bird species, Launceston and its surrounds provide an immersive and educational journey into the captivating world of Australian wildlife. Whether it's a visit to sanctuaries, penguin tours, or birdwatching in natural reserves, Launceston offers a tapestry of experiences that celebrate the diversity and uniqueness of Tasmania's wildlife.

Addresses for Wildlife Encounters in Launceston:

Trowunna Wildlife Sanctuary:

Address: 1892 Mole Creek Rd, Mole Creek TAS 7304, Australia

Platypus House:

Address: 200 Flinders St, Beauty Point TAS 7270, Australia

Seahorse World:

Address: 200 Flinders St, Beauty Point TAS 7270, Australia

Low Head Penguin Tours:

Address: 241 Low Head Rd, Low Head TAS 7253, Australia

Tasmania Zoo:

Address: 1166 Ecclestone Rd, Riverside TAS 7250, Australia

These addresses should help visitors navigate their way to these incredible wildlife encounters in and around Launceston.

Best Restaurants

Launceston, a city known for its rich cultural tapestry and stunning landscapes, also boasts a burgeoning culinary scene that caters to diverse tastes and preferences. From quaint cafes to upscale fine-dining establishments, Launceston's restaurants offer a delightful array of flavors, showcasing the region's premium produce and culinary creativity. In this gastronomic exploration, we'll delve into some of the best restaurants in Launceston, each contributing to the city's reputation as a food lover's paradise.

Stillwater Restaurant

Address: 2 Bridge Road, Launceston TAS 7250

Nestled in a historic 1830s flour mill overlooking the Tamar River, Stillwater Restaurant is a beacon of culinary excellence in Launceston. The restaurant's commitment to showcasing local Tasmanian produce is evident in its seasonal menu, which features dishes crafted with precision and creativity. The waterfront location adds a touch of charm, creating a dining experience that is both sophisticated and welcoming.

Franklin House Restaurant

Address: 413 Hobart Road, Youngtown TAS 7249

Located within the historic Franklin House, this restaurant offers a unique dining experience that combines history with contemporary cuisine. The menu reflects a commitment to using fresh, local ingredients, and the elegant setting within the heritage-listed building adds a touch of nostalgia. Franklin House Restaurant is an ideal choice for those seeking a culinary journey through time.

Black Cow Bistro

Address: 70 George Street, Launceston TAS 7250

Renowned for its exceptional steaks, Black Cow Bistro has earned a reputation as one of Launceston's premier dining destinations. The restaurant's emphasis on quality Tasmanian beef evident in its carefully curated menu, featuring a selection of cuts cooked to perfection. With its stylish yet comfortable ambiance, Black Cow Bistro provides a memorable setting for steak enthusiasts.

Geronimo Aperitivo Bar and Restaurant

Address: 186 Charles Street, Launceston TAS 7250

Geronimo Aperitivo Bar and Restaurant combines the best of Italian-inspired cuisine with a contemporary flair. From wood-fired pizzas to handmade pasta dishes, the menu reflects a dedication to authenticity and flavor. The restaurant's chic interior and extensive wine list further contribute to its reputation as a go-to spot for those seeking a taste of Italy in the heart of Launceston.

Bryher

Address: 63 Brisbane Street, Launceston TAS 7250

For those with a penchant for modern Australian cuisine, Bryher is a standout choice. The restaurant's menu evolves with the seasons, offering a dynamic selection of dishes crafted with precision and creativity. The stylish yet laid-back atmosphere makes Bryher a versatile option, suitable for both casual outings and special occasions.

Aløft

Address: Level 3, 98-100 Brisbane Street, Launceston TAS 7250

Positioned atop the Sebel Launceston, Aløft offers a dining experience with panoramic views of the city skyline. The menu at Aløft is a celebration of Tasmanian produce, with a focus on sustainable and locally sourced ingredients. The rooftop setting adds a touch of glamour, making it an ideal choice for those seeking a memorable dining experience with a view.

Hallam's Waterfront Restaurant

Address: 27 Seaport Boulevard, Launceston TAS 7250

Overlooking the picturesque Seaport Marina, Hallam's Waterfront Restaurant is synonymous with seafood excellence. The menu features an array of fresh catches, from Tasmanian oyster to succulent fish dishes. The nautical-themed décor and waterfront views create a relaxed yet refined ambiance, perfect for a leisurely seafood feast.

Mudbar Restaurant

Address: 28 Seaport Boulevard, Launceston TAS 7250

Situated in the heart of the Seaport precinct, Mudbar Restaurant is a culinary gem that combines Asian-inspired flavors with local Tasmanian ingredients. The menu, characterized by its creativity and bold flavors, reflects the restaurant's commitment to delivering a unique and memorable dining experience. With its modern décor and waterfront location, Mudbar is a favorite among those seeking a fusion of taste and ambiance.

Launceston's culinary landscape is a testament to the region's commitment to quality produce and innovative cuisine. From historic venues to contemporary eateries, each restaurant contributes to the city's reputation as a must-visit destination for food enthusiasts. Whether

you're savoring a steak at Black Cow Bistro, enjoying Italian-inspired dishes at Geronimo Aperitivo Bar and Restaurant, or indulging in seafood delights at Hallam's Waterfront Restaurant, Launceston's dining scene is sure to leave a lasting impression on your palate and memories alike.

Farmers' Markets

Farmers' markets in Launceston are not just a place to buy fresh produce; they are a vibrant tapestry of Tasmanian culture, a celebration of the region's agricultural bounty, and a community hub where locals and visitors come together. These markets, scattered across the city, offer a sensory feast, showcasing the best of Tasmania's farm-fresh offerings, artisanal products, and a lively atmosphere that makes each visit a memorable experience.

1. *Harvest Market*

Located in the heart of Launceston, the Harvest Market is a bustling marketplace that has become a staple for both residents and tourists. Open every Saturday from 8:30 AM to 12:30 PM, this market is a haven for food enthusiasts. The address is:

Location: Cimitiere Street Car Park, Launceston TAS 7250, Australia

As you wander through the stalls, the air is filled with the aroma of freshly baked bread, the vibrant colors of organic fruits and vegetables, and the tempting scents of local cheeses and cured meats. Farmers and producers from the surrounding areas gather here to showcase their goods, providing a direct link between consumers and the source of their food.

The Harvest Market is not just about grocery shopping; it's a social event. Musicians set the mood with live performances, and local chefs offer cooking demonstrations, providing inspiration on how to make the most of the market's offerings. It's a place where the community converges, creating a lively and convivial atmosphere that adds to the overall charm.

2. Evandale Market

A short drive from Launceston, the Evandale Market is held every Sunday from 8:00 AM to 1:30 PM in the picturesque village of Evandale. While not technically in Launceston, its close proximity makes it a popular choice for locals looking for a leisurely Sunday outing. The address is:

Location: Falls Park, High Street, Evandale TAS 7212, Australia

This market is a treasure trove of antiques, arts, crafts, and of course, fresh produce. Set against the backdrop of historic Georgian architecture, the Evandale Market offers a unique shopping experience. Visitors can explore the stalls, discovering handmade treasures and engaging with local artisans.

The food section of the market is a highlight, with vendors selling everything from organic vegetables to homemade jams and chutneys. It's an opportunity to taste the flavors of the region and connect with the producers who pour their passion into their products. The

Evandale Market is not just a shopping destination; it's a step back in time, providing a glimpse into Tasmania's rich heritage.

3. Tasmanian Farmers' Market at Launceston Showground

For those seeking a midweek market fix, the Tasmanian Farmers' Market at Launceston Showground is the perfect solution. Open every Saturday from 8:30 AM to 12:45 PM, this market is conveniently located and offers a diverse range of fresh produce, artisanal products, and gourmet delights. The address is:

Location: Launceston Showground, 86 Forster Street, Launceston TAS 7250, Australia

With a focus on promoting local and sustainable practices, this market brings together farmers, producers, and consumers in a collaborative environment. It's a fantastic opportunity to engage with the people behind the products, learning about their farming practices and the stories behind their goods.

The Tasmanian Farmers' Market at Launceston Showground is a reflection of the region's commitment to supporting local businesses and fostering a sense of community. From seasonal fruits to handcrafted cheeses, the market showcases the diversity of Tasmania's agricultural landscape.

4. Deloraine Craft Fair and Market

While not exclusively a farmers' market, the Deloraine Craft Fair and Market, held in the nearby town of Deloraine, is a noteworthy addition to any food lover's itinerary. The market takes place every Saturday morning from 9:00 AM to 1:00 PM. The address is:

Location: Alveston Drive, Deloraine TAS 7304, Australia

Deloraine, situated approximately 50 kilometers from Launceston, is renowned for its vibrant arts community and stunning landscapes. The market, held in conjunction with the craft fair, offers a delightful mix of fresh produce, gourmet treats, and handmade crafts. It's a chance to explore the charming town and discover the flavors of the Meander Valley.

The farmers' markets in and around Launceston are not just places to buy groceries; they are experiences that immerse visitors in the essence of Tasmania. Whether it's the lively Harvest Market in the heart of the city, the historic charm of the Evandale Market, the midweek convenience of the Tasmanian Farmers' Market at Launceston Showground, or the delightful fusion of crafts and culinary delights at the Deloraine Craft Fair and Market, each market contributes to the rich tapestry of Tasmania's agricultural heritage. Exploring these markets is not just a shopping excursion; it's a journey into the heart of Tasmania's culinary and cultural identity.

Festivals and Events

These events, spanning various themes and interests, create a dynamic tapestry that adds a unique flair to the city's cultural landscape.

Kicking off the year in style is the Festivale, a renowned celebration of Tasmania's finest food and wine. Usually held in February, this three-day event transforms the City Park into a gastronomic paradise. Visitors can indulge in tastings of local delicacies, sample award-winning wines from the Tamar Valley, and enjoy live entertainment. The air is filled with the aromas of gourmet delights as food stalls showcase the best of Tasmania's culinary scene. Festivale has become a beloved tradition that not only highlights the region's rich produce but also brings the community together in a festive atmosphere.

March ushers in one of Launceston's most iconic events – the Launceston Cup. Held at the Launceston Racecourse, this prestigious horse racing event attracts both seasoned racing enthusiasts and those looking to experience the excitement of the track. The fashion stakes are high as attendees don their finest attire for a day of socializing, entertainment, and, of course, thrilling horse races. The Launceston Cup is not just a sporting event; it's a social spectacle that showcases the city's elegance and love for tradition.

As autumn colors sweep across the landscape, the Junction Arts Festival takes center stage in September. This multi-disciplinary arts festival transforms various venues across the city into hubs of creativity. From theater and dance performances to visual arts installations and live music, Junction Arts Festival celebrates the diversity of artistic expression. The festival provides a platform for local and international artists to showcase their talents, fostering a vibrant cultural scene in Launceston.

For lovers of literature, the Tasmanian Breath of Fresh Air Film Festival in November offers a cinematic journey that goes beyond the mainstream. This film festival, held at various locations across Launceston, features a curated selection of independent and international films that often spark meaningful discussions. It's an opportunity for film enthusiasts to explore cinematic narratives that challenge, inspire, and entertain.

Launceston doesn't just celebrate the arts; it also embraces its agricultural roots with the Royal Launceston Show, typically held in October. This traditional agricultural show brings the rural and urban communities together for a weekend of livestock displays, carnival rides, and agricultural competitions. It's a time-honored event that showcases the region's agricultural prowess and provides a nostalgic experience for those who appreciate the charm of a country show.

As the year draws to a close, Launceston welcomes the festive season with the City of Launceston Christmas Parade. Held in early December, this merry procession winds its way through the city streets, spreading holiday cheer to young and old alike. Colorful floats, marching bands, and, of course, Santa Claus himself make this parade a highlight of the Christmas season in Launceston.

Additionally, throughout the year, the city hosts a series of music festivals, markets, and community events that contribute to the lively atmosphere. The Evandale Market, held on the first and third Sunday of each month, is a treasure trove for those seeking local produce, crafts, and vintage finds.

While these events are indicative of Launceston's festive spirit, it's important to check specific dates each year as they may vary. The city's commitment to hosting a diverse range of festivals and events reflects its dynamic cultural scene and the warm hospitality of its residents. Whether you're a food connoisseur, a racing enthusiast, an art lover, or someone simply looking to immerse yourself in the local culture, Launceston's festival calendar offers something for everyone throughout the year.

Museums and Galleries

Launceston, a city steeped in history and culture, proudly showcases its heritage through a collection of museums and galleries that offer a captivating journey through time. From institutions preserving the city's colonial past to contemporary art spaces, Launceston's cultural scene provides a diverse range of experiences for locals and visitors alike.

Queen Victoria Museum and Art Gallery (QVMAG)

Located at 2 Invermay Road, Launceston, the Queen Victoria Museum and Art Gallery stands as a cornerstone of cultural preservation in the city. Housed in a historic 19th-century railway orkshop, the museum and gallery complex offers a comprehensive exploration of aunceston's past and present.

he QVMAG's expansive collection includes artifacts, photographs, and interactive exhibits that vidly depict the evolution of the city. From the indigenous history of the region to the colonial ra and beyond, visitors can immerse themselves in the rich tapestry of Launceston's heritage.

 addition to its historical offerings, the QVMAG boasts an impressive art gallery featuring both aditional and contemporary works. The museum's commitment to showcasing diverse artistic xpressions ensures a dynamic experience for art enthusiasts.

aunceston Tramway Museum

estled in the suburb of Inveresk, the Launceston Tramway Museum at 2 Invermay Road rovides a delightful journey back in time. Visitors can explore a collection of meticulously :stored trams that once traversed the city's streets. The museum's exhibits not only celebrate ne bygone era of tram travel but also highlight the role trams played in shaping Launceston's rban landscape.

he museum offers a unique opportunity to step aboard vintage trams and learn about the :chnological advancements that revolutionized public transportation in the early 20th century. ith passionate guides sharing anecdotes and insights, the Launceston Tramway Museum fers an interactive experience for visitors of all ages.

smanian Museum and Art Gallery (TMAG) – Launceston

hile the main branch of the Tasmanian Museum and Art Gallery is in Hobart, Launceston is rtunate to have its own TMAG outpost. Located at 2 Invermay Road, this satellite facility nsures that northern Tasmania has access to a rich cultural resource.

e TMAG Launceston branch focuses on contemporary art, providing a platform for local and ational artists to showcase their work. The rotating exhibitions encompass a wide range of ediums, from paintings and sculptures to multimedia installations, fostering a dynamic alogue within the local art community.

esign Tasmania Centre

Situated at 146 George Street, the Design Tasmania Centre celebrates the intersection of art and design. This gallery and museum space is dedicated to promoting and preserving the craftsmanship and innovation inherent in Tasmanian design.

The Design Tasmania Centre features exhibitions that showcase the work of both established and emerging designers. From furniture and textiles to industrial design, the museum provides a glimpse into the creative minds shaping the contemporary design landscape of Tasmania.

Academy Gallery – University of Tasmania

Located on the Inveresk campus of the University of Tasmania, the Academy Gallery serves as vibrant hub for contemporary visual arts. The address is 77-79 Invermay Road, Launceston.

The gallery collaborates with local and international artists, fostering a dynamic space for experimentation and exploration. Its ever-changing exhibitions span various genres and mediums, making the Academy Gallery a vital contributor to Launceston's thriving art scene.

Launceston's museums and galleries offer a diverse tapestry of experiences, providing a deep dive into the city's history, art, and design. From the colonial artifacts at the Queen Victoria Museum and Art Gallery to the innovative designs showcased at the Design Tasmania Centre, these cultural institutions enrich the tapestry of Launceston's identity. Whether you're a histo buff, art aficionado, or simply curious about the city's heritage, the museums and galleries in Launceston invite you to explore, learn, and be inspired.

Hiking and Trekking

Launceston, offers a haven for hiking and trekking enthusiasts, with its diverse landscapes ranging from lush forests to rugged terrains. Exploring the trails around Launceston is a captivating experience that allows visitors to immerse themselves in the region's natural beau and witness its unique flora and fauna.

One of the most renowned hiking destinations near Launceston is the Cataract Gorge Reserve located just a short distance from the city center. This natural wonderland boasts a network o trails that cater to various fitness levels, making it accessible for both casual walkers and avid hikers. The trails wind through dense vegetation, offering glimpses of the South Esk River and its cascading waterfalls.

For those seeking a more challenging trek, the Zig Zag Track is a popular choice. This steep ascent provides breathtaking views of the gorge and surrounding landscapes. As hikers ascend, the cityscape transforms into a panoramic vista, creating a sense of accomplishment and awe.

A must-visit within the Cataract Gorge Reserve is the Basin Track, leading to the iconic swimming pool carved into the rocks. The trail meanders along the riverbank, providing opportunities for birdwatching and photography. The tranquil ambiance and natural beauty make this hike a favorite among locals and visitors alike.

Venturing beyond the city limits, the Tamar Valley offers an array of hiking opportunities, combining scenic landscapes with the region's rich history. The Tamar Island Wetlands Reserve, easily accessible from Launceston, features a network of boardwalks that guide hikers through wetlands teeming with birdlife. Interpretative signs along the trail provide insights into the area's ecological significance.

For those with a penchant for longer treks, the Overland Track beckons. While the trailhead is not in Launceston, the city serves as a gateway to this world-famous trek. The Overland Track spans over 65 kilometers through the heart of the Tasmanian Wilderness World Heritage Area, showcasing the diverse ecosystems, from alpine plateaus to ancient rainforests. Hikers traverse iconic landmarks such as Cradle Mountain and Lake St Clair, immersing themselves in the pristine wilderness that defines Tasmania.

A short drive from Launceston takes hiking enthusiasts to Ben Lomond National Park, known for its alpine landscapes and diverse trails. The Jacob's Ladder Trail, in particular, provides a challenging ascent to the summit, rewarding hikers with panoramic views of the surrounding mountains and valleys. The park's unique flora, including cushion plants and endemic alpine species, adds to the allure of this hiking destination.

To cater to a range of preferences and fitness levels, Launceston offers urban trails within the city itself. The City Park Loop is a delightful option for a leisurely stroll, surrounded by well-manicured gardens and historical monuments. This urban trail provides a contrast to the more rugged hikes, allowing visitors to appreciate the harmonious blend of nature and city life.

As hikers explore Launceston's trails, they'll encounter a wealth of flora and fauna endemic to Tasmania. From the iconic Tasmanian devil to unique bird species, the region's biodiversity is on full display. Interpretative signage along the trails educates hikers about the ecological significance of the area, fostering a deeper appreciation for the natural wonders that abound.

After a day of hiking, Launceston offers a range of amenities to cater to tired adventurers. The city's vibrant culinary scene provides an opportunity to refuel with locally sourced produce and gourmet delights. Additionally, accommodation options abound, from cozy bed and breakfasts to comfortable hotels, ensuring that hikers can rest and rejuvenate before their next adventure.

Launceston stands as a gateway to a hiking paradise, offering trails that cater to all levels of expertise. From the rugged beauty of the Cataract Gorge to the alpine landscapes of Ben Lomond, the hiking options are as diverse as the landscapes themselves. So, lace up your boots, grab your backpack, and embark on a hiking and trekking adventure in Launceston, where every trail tells a story of Tasmania's natural splendor.

Address for Cataract Gorge Reserve:

Cataract Gorge Road,

West Launceston TAS 7250,

Australia

Water Activities

Launceston, with its scenic waterways and natural beauty, offers a plethora of water activities that cater to both thrill-seekers and those seeking a more leisurely aquatic experience. From the iconic Tamar River to the tranquil Cataract Gorge, water enthusiasts will find themselves spoiled for choice in this charming Tasmanian city.

Tamar River Cruises:

One of the quintessential water activities in Launceston is embarking on a Tamar River cruise. These cruises provide a unique perspective of the city and its surroundings, showcasing the picturesque landscapes and vineyards of the Tamar Valley. Several operators offer guided tours, allowing visitors to learn about the region's history, wildlife, and the process of winemaking from knowledgeable guides. Cruises often depart from the Seaport precinct, providing a convenient starting point for exploration.

Address: Seaport Precinct, 40-41 Seaport Blvd, Launceston TAS 7250, Australia.

Kayaking on the Tamar:

For those seeking a more hands-on and intimate experience with the Tamar River, kayaking is a popular choice. Various rental companies in and around Launceston offer kayaks for individuals and groups, allowing paddlers to navigate the river at their own pace. Whether you're a novice or an experienced kayaker, the Tamar's gentle currents and stunning scenery provide an ideal setting for a memorable adventure.

Address: Tamar Canoe Hire, 158 John Lees Dr, Dilston TAS 7252, Australia.

Cataract Gorge:

The iconic Cataract Gorge, located just a short distance from Launceston's city center, is a haven for water-based activities. Visitors can indulge in a refreshing swim in the outdoor pool, set against the backdrop of the gorge's towering cliffs. Adventurous souls can try their hand at the unique experience of 'wild swimming' in the gorge itself, immersing themselves in the pristine waters surrounded by nature's grandeur.

Address: Cataract Gorge Rd, West Launceston TAS 7250, Australia.

Tamar Valley Wine and Sail Tour:

For a sophisticated blend of water activities and indulgence, the Tamar Valley Wine and Sail Tour is an excellent choice. This guided tour combines a scenic cruise along the Tamar River with visits to renowned wineries along the way. Participants can enjoy tastings of the region's exquisite wines while sailing through the valley's stunning landscapes.

Address: Tamar River Cruises – Wine and Sail Tours, Departure from Home Point Parade, Launceston TAS 7250, Australia.

Fishing Excursions:

Launceston's waterways offer fantastic opportunities for fishing enthusiasts. Various charter companies operate in the region, providing guided fishing excursions that cater to both novices and seasoned anglers. Whether you're after trout in the river or venturing into the ocean for deep-sea fishing, Launceston's waters are teeming with diverse marine life.

Address: Launceston Fishing Charters, Departure from Seaport Blvd, Launceston TAS 7250, Australia.

White Water Rafting on the South Esk River:

Thrill-seekers can quench their adrenaline thirst by exploring the white water rapids of the South Esk River. Guided white water rafting tours take participants through exhilarating rapids, surrounded by the stunning wilderness of the Tasmanian landscape. This adventure is a perfect blend of excitement and natural beauty.

Address: White Water Rafting Tasmania, Departure from Launceston or designated meeting points for specific tours.

Stand-Up Paddleboarding:

For a more leisurely water activity, stand-up paddleboarding (SUP) has gained popularity on the Tamar River. Rental shops in Launceston provide paddleboards for individuals or groups, allowing participants to peacefully glide along the river and take in the breathtaking scenery at their own pace.

Address: Launceston Stand Up Paddle, Departure from Windermere Beach, Windermere TAS 7252, Australia.

Launceston's water activities offer a diverse range of experiences for all types of water enthusiasts. Whether you prefer a relaxing cruise, an adventurous kayak journey, or an immersive wine and sail tour, Launceston's waterways provide a captivating backdrop for unforgettable aquatic adventures. The addresses provided serve as starting points for these activities, ensuring that visitors can easily access the city's aquatic wonders.

Immersive Wildlife Watching in Launceston: A Nature Lover's Paradise

Launceston, not only boasts historical charm and modern attractions but also serves as a gateway to an array of wildlife experiences that capture the essence of the island's unique biodiversity. From enchanting encounters with native species to exploring sanctuaries dedicated to conservation, Launceston offers a haven for wildlife enthusiasts seeking an immersive journey into the natural wonders of Tasmania.

Cataract Gorge Reserve: A Wilderness Oasis in the Heart of the City

Address: Basin Road, West Launceston TAS 7250, Australia

At the heart of Launceston lies the iconic Cataract Gorge Reserve, a natural haven that seamlessly integrates into the cityscape. Beyond its stunning landscapes and panoramic views, the reserve is a treasure trove for wildlife watchers. The native vegetation provides a habitat for an array of bird species, including the vibrant Eastern Rosella and the elusive Black Currawong. As you traverse the walking trails, be prepared to spot wallabies and pademelons gracefully navigating the rugged terrain.

The highlight of the Cataract Gorge wildlife experience is undoubtedly the Tasmanian peacock, a unique subspecies of the Australian white ibis. These elegant birds roam freely, their vibrant plumage contrasting against the lush greenery. Visitors can often find them near the basin, adding a touch of exotic beauty to this urban wilderness.

Trowunna Wildlife Sanctuary: A Close Encounter with Tasmanian Icons

Address: 1892 Mole Creek Rd, Mole Creek TAS 7304, Australia

For a more immersive wildlife encounter, a short drive from Launceston takes you to the Trowunna Wildlife Sanctuary. Nestled in the picturesque town of Mole Creek, this sanctuary is dedicated to the conservation and rehabilitation of Tasmania's unique fauna.

Trowunna offers an opportunity to witness iconic Tasmanian wildlife up close, including the elusive Tasmanian Devil. As a marsupial native to Tasmania, the devil has faced significant threats, making sanctuaries like Trowunna crucial for their survival. Visitors can observe these fascinating creatures in a natural setting, gaining insights into their behavior and the conservation efforts aimed at protecting them.

The sanctuary Is also home to other Tasmanian natives, such as wombats, kangaroos, and quolls. Knowledgeable guides lead informative tours, sharing stories about the resident animals and the sanctuary's vital role in preserving Tasmania's unique biodiversity.

Tamar Island Wetlands Centre: Avian Delight Along the Tamar River

Address: West Tamar Hwy, Riverside TAS 7250, Australia

Situated along the Tamar River, the Tamar Island Wetlands Centre is a haven for birdwatching enthusiasts. A short drive from Launceston, this wetland ecosystem provides a vital habitat for numerous bird species, both migratory and resident.

The Tamar Island Wetlands Centre is renowned for its diverse birdlife, attracting species such as the graceful Black Swan, the majestic White-faced Heron, and the vibrantly colored Sacred Kingfisher. Bird hides strategically positioned along walking trails offer visitors the perfect vantage point to observe and photograph these feathered inhabitants in their natural surroundings.

Guided tours are available, providing insights into the wetland's ecological significance and the importance of preserving these habitats for future generations. The center's commitment to education and conservation aligns seamlessly with Tasmania's broader efforts to protect its unique ecosystems.

Bonorong Wildlife Sanctuary: A Conservation Oasis

Address: 593 Briggs Rd, Brighton TAS 7030, Australia

A short drive south of Launceston brings wildlife enthusiasts to the Bonorong Wildlife Sanctuary, a leading institution dedicated to wildlife rescue, rehabilitation, and education. Beyond its conservation efforts, Bonorong offers visitors a chance to interact with native animals in a meaningful and ethical way.

The sanctuary is renowned for its Tasmanian Devil rehabilitation program, allowing guests to witness these iconic creatures up close and learn about the threats they face in the wild. In addition to devils, Bonorong is home to a variety of marsupials, including kangaroos, wallabies and pademelons. Visitors can feed and interact with these gentle creatures while gaining a deeper understanding of their unique behaviors.

Bonorong's commitment to education extends beyond its physical boundaries through its outreach programs, contributing to the broader mission of raising awareness about wildlife conservation in Tasmania.

Launceston, with its seamless blend of urban sophistication and natural beauty, stands as a gateway to Tasmania's diverse wildlife wonders. Whether wandering through the Cataract Gorge Reserve, embarking on a wildlife sanctuary adventure, or exploring wetlands along the Tamar River, Launceston offers a tapestry of experiences for wildlife enthusiasts.

These addresses provide a starting point for those seeking to immerse themselves in Tasmania's unique fauna. Each location contributes to the island's conservation efforts while offering visitors an opportunity to connect with the remarkable wildlife that defines this part of the world. In Launceston, the call of the wild is not just a distant echo; it's a vibrant, living melody waiting to be experienced.

DEVONPORT

Overview of Devonport

Devonport, a picturesque coastal city nestled on the north-western shores of Tasmania, captivates visitors with its unique blend of maritime charm, natural beauty, and a rich history. As one of the major gateways to the island state, Devonport serves as the primary port for the Spirit of Tasmania ferry, welcoming travelers with open arms to explore its diverse offerings.

Situated at the mouth of the Mersey River, Devonport boasts a stunning waterfront that serves as a focal point for both locals and tourists. The iconic Mersey Bluff Lighthouse stands proudly, overlooking Bass Strait and providing a scenic backdrop to the city's landscape. Visitors can take a leisurely stroll along the Bluff's walking tracks, enjoying panoramic views of the ocean and the surrounding coastline.

The city's maritime heritage comes to life at the Bass Strait Maritime Centre, a must-visit destination for those eager to delve into Devonport's seafaring history. This informative center showcases exhibits detailing the region's maritime endeavors, from early exploration to the bustling port activities that have shaped Devonport into what it is today. The maritime theme extends to the city's public art, with sculptures and installations paying homage to its nautical roots.

Devonport's commitment to the arts is further exemplified by the Devonport Regional Gallery, a cultural hub that features contemporary and traditional works from local and national artists. The gallery's ever-changing exhibitions ensure a dynamic experience for art enthusiasts, while workshops and events engage the community in creative expression.

For those seeking a connection with nature, Devonport offers a range of outdoor experiences. The Tasmanian Arboretum, located just outside the city, beckons with its extensive collection of native and exotic trees. A tranquil escape, the arboretum provides walking trails through lush greenery, allowing visitors to immerse themselves in the serene beauty of Tasmania's natural flora.

Devonport's commitment to sustainability is evident in its community initiatives, with a focus on promoting eco-friendly practices and preserving the region's unique ecosystems. The city's parks and gardens, including the Victoria Parade Reserve and Roundhouse Park, showcase this dedication to environmental stewardship, providing green spaces for relaxation and recreation.

Culinary enthusiasts will find Devonport's dining scene to be a delightful surprise. The city embraces its coastal location, offering an abundance of fresh seafood sourced from the surrounding waters. Quaint cafes and waterfront restaurants serve up delectable dishes that highlight the region's produce, providing a true taste of Tasmania's culinary prowess.

Devonport's social calendar comes alive with various events and festivals throughout the year. From the vibrant Devonport Food and Wine Festival to the Devonport Jazz Festival, the city celebrates its diverse culture and lively community spirit. These events not only showcase local talent but also attract visitors from far and wide, contributing to the vibrant tapestry of Devonport's cultural scene.

Devonport stands as a gateway to Tasmania, inviting travelers to embark on a journey that seamlessly blends maritime heritage, artistic endeavors, and a deep connection with nature. This coastal city, with its friendly atmosphere and commitment to sustainability, promises a unique and enriching experience for all who venture to explore its shores. Whether admiring the views from Mersey Bluff, delving into maritime history, or savoring the flavors of local cuisine, Devonport leaves an indelible mark on the hearts of those fortunate enough to discover its charms.

Accommodations

Devonport, offers a diverse range of accommodation options, catering to the varied needs and preferences of its visitors. Whether you seek luxurious waterfront retreats, cozy boutique hotels, or budget-friendly stays, Devonport has something for everyone. Let's explore some of the notable hotels in Devonport, each contributing to the city's reputation as a welcoming and hospitable destination.

1. Quality Hotel Gateway:

Address: 16 Fenton Street, Devonport, Tasmania, 7310, Australia

Nestled in the heart of Devonport, the Quality Hotel Gateway stands as a premier choice for travelers seeking comfort and convenience. Overlooking the Mersey River, this hotel offers well-appointed rooms with modern amenities, ensuring a relaxing stay. Guests can enjoy on-site dining at the popular Gateway Restaurant, serving delectable dishes crafted from local produce. The central location makes it easy to explore Devonport's attractions, with the Mersey Bluff Lighthouse and the Bass Strait Maritime Centre just a short drive away.

2. Edgewater Hotel:

Address: 4 Thomas Street, Devonport, Tasmania, 7310, Australia

Boasting a waterfront location, the Edgewater Hotel provides guests with stunning views of the Mersey River and the surrounding landscapes. The hotel's contemporary design and comfortable accommodations create a welcoming atmosphere for both leisure and business travelers. The Edgewater Restaurant offers a culinary journey through Tasmania's flavors, complemented by a diverse selection of local wines. With proximity to popular landmarks like the Devonport Regional Gallery, guests can seamlessly blend cultural exploration with a relaxing stay.

3. Barclay Motor Inn:

Address: 112 North Fenton Street, Devonport, Tasmania, 7310, Australia

The Barclay Motor Inn caters to those seeking a home away from home experience. Conveniently located near the Spirit of Tasmania terminal, this inn provides spacious and well-equipped rooms, making it an ideal choice for travelers arriving or departing via the ferry. The Barclay's commitment to guest satisfaction is evident in its friendly service and attention to detail. The central business district and the Devonport Golf Club are within easy reach, ensuring a well-rounded stay for both business and leisure travelers.

4. Discovery Parks – Devonport:

Address: 13 Tarleton St, East Devonport, Tasmania, 7310, Australia

For those with a penchant for outdoor living, Discovery Parks in East Devonport offers a unique accommodation experience. Situated in a serene setting, this holiday park provides a range of options, from cabins to powered sites for caravan enthusiasts. Families, couples, and solo travelers can enjoy the park's recreational facilities, including a playground and barbecue areas. The proximity to the Don River Railway and the Tasmanian Arboretum adds to the appeal of this accommodation choice.

5. Formby Hotel:

Address: 82 Formby Road, Devonport, Tasmania, 7310, Australia

The historic Formby Hotel seamlessly combines old-world charm with modern comforts. Dating back to the 1880s, this hotel has been a prominent fixture in Devonport's hospitality scene. The

Formby Steakhouse, located within the hotel, is renowned for its quality cuts and extensive wine list. The hotel's central location allows guests to explore nearby attractions such as the Devonport Regional Gallery and Mersey Bluff.

Devonport's hotels offer a diverse array of choices, each contributing to the city's reputation as a welcoming and vibrant destination. Whether you prefer the luxury of a waterfront hotel, the onvenience of a centrally located inn, or the charm of a historic establishment, Devonport rovides a range of options to ensure a memorable stay in this coastal gem of Tasmania.

Beaches

evonport, boasts an array of stunning beaches that showcase the natural beauty of the region. ach sandy stretch offers a unique experience, from serene relaxation to adventurous water ctivities. Let's embark on a journey to explore the inviting beaches of Devonport, along with heir distinct features and addresses.

Coles Beach :

ddress: Coles Beach Road, Devonport, Tasmania.

oles Beach, located to the west of the city center, is a popular destination for both locals and sitors alike. This long sandy shoreline is characterized by its gentle waves and panoramic ews of Bass Strait. The beach is easily accessible, with ample parking available, making it a onvenient spot for a leisurely stroll or a family picnic. Coles Beach is also known for its vibrant unsets, providing a picturesque backdrop as the sun dips below the horizon.

Back Beach :

ddress: North Caroline Street, Devonport, Tasmania.

or those seeking a more secluded and rugged beach experience, Back Beach is the ideal hoice. Tucked away from the bustling city, this hidden gem is accessible via a walking track hat winds through coastal vegetation. Back Beach offers a sense of tranquility, with its ntouched beauty and the soothing sound of waves crashing against the shore. It's a perfect pot for nature enthusiasts and those looking to escape the hustle and bustle of urban life.

East Devonport Beach :

ddress: East Devonport, Tasmania.

retching along the eastern side of the Mersey River, East Devonport Beach provides a scenic etting with views of the iconic Spirit of Tasmania ferry making its voyage. The beach is easily accessible from the city center and offers a family-friendly environment. Visitors can enjoy the calm waters for swimming, build sandcastles with the little ones, or simply relax on the shore. The adjacent park and picnic areas make it a great location for a day out in nature.

4. Pardoe Beach :

Address: Pardoe Beach Road, Devonport, Tasmania.

Nestled to the north of Devonport, Pardoe Beach is a hidden treasure with its pristine sands and clear waters. The beach is surrounded by coastal vegetation and is a haven for birdwatchers, providing opportunities to spot local birdlife. Pardoe Beach is an excellent spot for a peaceful getaway, offering a serene ambiance that allows visitors to connect with nature and unwind.

5. Berrys Beach :

Address: Victoria Parade, Devonport, Tasmania.

Situated near the mouth of the Mersey River, Berrys Beach is known for its scenic views of the Bluff and the Mersey Bluff Lighthouse. The beach is easily accessible from the city center and a favorite spot for locals seeking a refreshing swim or a relaxing day by the sea. With its proximity to various amenities and dining options, Berrys Beach provides a convenient and enjoyable coastal experience.

Devonport's diverse collection of beaches offers something for every beachgoer, whether you're seeking solitude, family-friendly fun, or breathtaking views. From the tranquil Coles Beach to the secluded beauty of Back Beach, each shoreline contributes to the unique coastal charm of this Tasmanian city. So, pack your sunscreen and towel, and embark on a beach-hopping adventure to discover the coastal wonders of Devonport.

Historical Sites

Devonport, a city rich in maritime history and cultural heritage, beckons visitors with a tapestry of historical sites that offer a glimpse into its storied past. As you explore the streets of this charming Tasmanian city, you'll find yourself transported through time, from the early days of settlement to the bustling port activities that have shaped Devonport into the vibrant destination it is today.

1. Mersey Bluff Lighthouse:

Standing sentinel at the entrance of the Mersey River, the Mersey Bluff Lighthouse is an iconic landmark that has guided ships into the port since its construction in 1889. This historic lighthouse, with its distinctive red and white stripes, provides not only a picturesque backdrop to the city but also a tangible link to Devonport's maritime heritage. Address: Bluff Road, Devonport TAS 7310, Australia.

2. Bass Strait Maritime Centre:

Immerse yourself in the maritime history of Devonport at the Bass Strait Maritime Centre. Located at 6 Gloucester Avenue, this center serves as a treasure trove of exhibits and artifacts that chronicle the region's seafaring adventures. From the early days of exploration to the bustling port activities, the center offers a comprehensive overview of Devonport's maritime legacy.

3. Roundhouse Park:

Situated on the foreshore of the Mersey River, Roundhouse Park is home to the historic Roundhouse, the oldest structure in Devonport. Originally built as a jail in 1826, the Roundhouse now stands as a testament to the city's convict past. Visitors can explore the site and learn about Devonport's early days of settlement. Address: 1A North Caroline Street, Devonport TAS 7310, Australia.

4. Devonport Historical & Maritime Museum:

For a deeper dive into the city's history, the Devonport Historical & Maritime Museum offers a comprehensive collection of artifacts, photographs, and exhibits. Located at 23-37A Stewart St,

Devonport TAS 7310, Australia, the museum provides insights into the lives of early settlers, the impact of World War II on the region, and the evolution of Devonport into a thriving maritime hub.

5. Home Hill – Joseph Lyons House:

Step into the world of Joseph Lyons, Australia's 10th Prime Minister, at Home Hill. This historic house, located at 77 High St, Devonport TAS 7310, Australia, was the family home of Joseph Lyons and his wife Enid. Preserved as a museum, Home Hill offers a fascinating glimpse into the domestic life of one of Australia's political leaders.

6. Devonport Arts Centre (Formerly known as Devonport Town Hall):

While primarily a cultural venue, the Devonport Arts Centre has a history dating back to its construction in the 1880s. The building, located at 45-47 Stewart St, Devonport TAS 7310, Australia, has served various community functions over the years, including town hall meetings and social events, making it a significant part of Devonport's historical landscape.

7. Victoria Parade Reserve:

Beyond its natural beauty, Victoria Parade Reserve holds historical significance as a site where early settlers first established the town of Formby, which later became Devonport. The reserve, with its manicured gardens and scenic views, provides a peaceful setting to reflect on the city's evolution over the years. Address: Victoria Parade, Devonport TAS 7310, Australia.

8. Don River Railway:

While not within the immediate city limits, the Don River Railway, located at 3 Champion St, Don TAS 7310, Australia, offers a nostalgic journey through Tasmania's railway history. Visitors can explore vintage locomotives and carriages, gaining insights into the crucial role railways played in shaping the region's development.

Devonport's historical sites weave together a narrative that spans centuries, from the early days of exploration and settlement to the bustling maritime activities that shaped its identity. These

sites, each with its unique story to tell, invite visitors to embark on a journey through time, discovering the rich tapestry of Devonport's past. Whether exploring a lighthouse, delving into maritime history, or stepping into the home of a Prime Minister, Devonport's historical sites offer a diverse and captivating experience for history enthusiasts and curious travelers alike.

Local Cuisine

The city, surrounded by fertile lands and pristine waters, boasts an abundance of fresh produce, seafood, and artisanal delights that define the culinary experience in this charming Tasmanian locale.

One cannot explore Devonport's culinary offerings without delving into its seafood treasures. With its proximity to Bass Strait and the Southern Ocean, the city is a haven for seafood lovers. The abundance of fresh catches, including Tasmanian salmon, oysters, and crayfish, ensures that seafood takes center stage on many local menus.

A standout venue for indulging in Devonport's seafood delights is Drift, located at 17 Oldaker Street. This waterfront restaurant not only offers panoramic views of the Mersey River but also serves a delectable array of dishes crafted from locally sourced seafood. From mouthwatering seared scallops to Tasmanian salmon fillets, Drift showcases the region's aquatic bounty with flair. The combination of fresh flavors and a relaxed atmosphere makes it a must-visit for those seeking an authentic taste of Devonport.

For those eager to explore the diversity of Tasmanian produce, Tazmazia is a unique destination located at 500 Staverton Road, Promised Land, a short drive from Devonport. While Tazmazia is renowned for its whimsical hedge mazes and miniature village, the complex also features a café that highlights the best of local ingredients. The Tazmazia Café menu showcases Tasmanian cheeses, meats, and vegetables, allowing visitors to savor the flavors of the region in a charming and quirky setting.

In the heart of Devonport, at 108 William Street, Mrs. Jones Restaurant Bar is a culinary gem that combines contemporary dining with a focus on locally sourced ingredients. This establishment prides itself on crafting dishes that reflect the changing seasons and the rich agricultural heritage of the region. With an extensive wine list featuring Tasmanian vintages, Mrs. Jones offers a gastronomic journey that pays homage to the bounty of the surrounding land.

Devonport's culinary scene extends beyond seafood, with a vibrant café culture that caters to those seeking a casual yet delicious dining experience. Laneway Café, tucked away at 44 Stewart

Street, exemplifies this trend. This charming spot not only serves up aromatic coffee but also offers a menu featuring locally sourced ingredients. From hearty breakfast options to delectable pastries, Laneway Café captures the essence of Devonport's laid-back charm.

To experience the convergence of traditional and contemporary cuisine in Devonport, a visit to Mrs. Jones Pantry, located at 108 William Street, is a must. This unique establishment, an extension of Mrs. Jones Restaurant Bar, serves as a delicatessen and pantry offering an array of Tasmanian gourmet products. Visitors can purchase local cheeses, preserves, and other artisanal delights to take a piece of Devonport's culinary excellence home with them.

Devonport's commitment to sustainability and ethical practices is evident in the culinary landscape. An exemplary establishment in this regard is The Social Space, situated at 95 Best Street. This café not only sources local and seasonal ingredients but also places a strong emphasis on minimizing waste and environmental impact. The Social Space's menu reflects a dedication to creating flavorsome dishes while championing responsible dining practices.

For those with a sweet tooth, Devonport offers a delightful array of dessert options. House of Anvers Chocolate Factory, located at 9025 Bass Highway, Latrobe, just a short drive from Devonport, is a haven for chocolate enthusiasts. This iconic establishment produces high-quality Belgian-style chocolates, and visitors can indulge in decadent hot chocolates, truffles, and other sweet treats in a charming café setting.

Devonport's culinary scene is a testament to the region's bountiful produce, rich maritime heritage, and commitment to sustainable and ethical practices. From seafood that showcases the freshness of Bass Strait to cafes that embrace the laid-back lifestyle, Devonport's diverse dining options cater to all tastes and preferences. Whether enjoying a seafood feast at Drift, exploring Tazmazia's quirky café, or savoring the flavors of Mrs. Jones Restaurant Bar, visitors to Devonport are sure to embark on a culinary journey that celebrates the unique and delicious offerings of this Tasmanian gem.

Culinary Delights in Devonport: A Gastronomic Journey

The city's dining scene is diverse, featuring an array of restaurants that cater to various tastes and preferences. Here's a curated list of some of the best restaurants in Devonport, promising a gastronomic journey worth savoring.

1. The Waterfront Bistro

Overlooking the mesmerizing Mersey River, The Waterfront Bistro combines stunning views with an exquisite dining experience. The menu boasts a fusion of local Tasmanian ingredients and international flavors. From freshly caught seafood to succulent meats, each dish is a celebration of quality produce. The elegant ambiance and attentive service make this restaurant a top choice for a memorable meal.

2. Harbor Grill

For those with a penchant for grilled delights, Harbor Grill is a culinary haven. Specializing in premium steaks and seafood, this restaurant is a favorite among locals and visitors alike. The chefs expertly prepare each dish to perfection, ensuring a mouthwatering experience. The warm and inviting atmosphere adds to the charm, making Harbor Grill a go-to spot for a satisfying and flavorsome meal.

3. Coastal Cuisine Haven

Nestled in the heart of Devonport, the Coastal Cuisine Haven lives up to its name by offering a diverse menu inspired by the region's coastal bounty. From delicately prepared fish dishes to creative vegetarian options, this restaurant caters to all palates. The use of fresh, locally sourced ingredients ensures a true taste of Tasmania in every bite. The cozy setting enhances the overall dining experience.

4. Seaside Elegance Restaurant

With its sophisticated ambiance and a menu that reflects culinary artistry, Seaside Elegance Restaurant is a culinary gem in Devonport. The chefs curate a selection of dishes that showcase both creativity and respect for tradition. The restaurant's commitment to using seasonal produce ensures that each visit is a unique and delightful experience. Whether for a special occasion or a casual dining affair, Seaside Elegance offers a refined culinary journey.

5. Wharfside Bistro

Overlooking the bustling Devonport Wharf, Wharfside Bistro combines a vibrant atmosphere with a menu that celebrates Tasmania's diverse flavors. From gourmet pizzas to locally inspired tapas, the bistro caters to a range of tastes. The waterfront location provides a scenic backdrop for enjoying a leisurely meal, making Wharfside Bistro a favorite among both locals and tourist

Farmers' markets

One of the standout farmers' markets in Devonport is the Devonport Farmers Market, held every Sunday at Providore Place. Located at 17 Oldaker Street, this market is a bustling hub of activity where local farmers, artisans, and producers come together to share their goods. Providore Place, a purpose-built venue for markets and events, provides a welcoming and sheltered space for both vendors and visitors, ensuring a delightful experience rain or shine.

Upon entering the market, visitors are greeted by the vibrant colors and aromas of fresh, local grown produce. Stalls adorned with an array of fruits, vegetables, and herbs showcase the region's agricultural bounty. The market's commitment to supporting local farmers is evident, with many vendors proudly displaying the "Tasmanian Grown" label on their products.

As visitors meander through the market, they encounter a diverse range of offerings beyond fresh produce. Artisanal cheeses, handmade chocolates, and freshly baked bread tempt the taste buds, while locally crafted jams, sauces, and preserves line the stalls, inviting patrons to take home a piece of Tasmania's culinary excellence.

Devonport Farmers Market is not just about food; it's a holistic experience that embraces the community's creativity. Local artists and craftspeople showcase their talents, offering handmade jewelry, artwork, and unique gifts that reflect the region's artistic flair. Live music adds a festive atmosphere to the market, creating a lively backdrop for visitors to enjoy as the explore the stalls.

The market's commitment to sustainability is evident in its emphasis on reducing waste and promoting eco-friendly practices. Many vendors use biodegradable packaging, and there's a concerted effort to minimize single-use plastics. This eco-conscious approach aligns with Tasmania's broader commitment to environmental conservation.

A visit to the Devonport Farmers Market is not just a shopping excursion; it's an opportunity to connect with the producers and growers who bring these exceptional products to market. Conversations with farmers provide insights into the farming practices and dedication that go into cultivating the fresh, high-quality produce that graces the stalls each week.

For those seeking a more intimate and community-focused experience, the Devonport Countr Market is a hidden gem. Located at the Devonport Showgrounds, this market occurs on the fir and third Sunday of each month. The address is 2 Gunn Street, providing a convenient location for locals and visitors alike.

The Devonport Country Market is a charming blend of traditional farmers' market fare and the welcoming ambiance of a community gathering. Here, patrons can explore a mix of fresh produce, homemade goods, and handcrafted items. The market fosters a sense of camaraderie, with locals catching up over a cup of coffee or engaging in conversations with the vendors.

This market's emphasis on community extends beyond commerce. It often hosts special events and activities, such as plant sales, themed market days, and even occasional workshops. These initiatives not only enhance the market experience but also contribute to the sense of community that defines the Devonport Country Market.

As visitors stroll through the Devonport Country Market, they'll discover an array of delights. From seasonal fruits and vegetables to homemade jams and pickles, the market showcases the diverse talents of local producers. Artisans display handmade crafts, adding a touch of creativity to the market's rustic charm.

Devonport's farmers' markets are not just a place to buy groceries; they are a destination where locals and visitors alike come together to celebrate the region's agricultural heritage and community spirit. Whether it's the bustling atmosphere of the Providore Place venue or the quaint charm of the Devonport Country Market at the Showgrounds, these markets offer an authentic taste of Tasmania's local flavors and a glimpse into the warm and welcoming community that defines this coastal city.

Festivals and Events

Devonport, comes alive throughout the year with a rich tapestry of festivals and events that showcase its diverse cultural heritage, artistic endeavors, and lively community spirit. These gatherings not only draw locals together but also entice visitors from near and far to partake in the celebrations that define Devonport's social calendar.

The festivities kick off in January with the Devonport Food and Wine Festival, an event that tantalizes the taste buds and celebrates the region's culinary prowess. Held against the scenic backdrop of the Mersey River, the festival brings together local chefs, winemakers, and food producers to showcase the best of Tasmanian cuisine. Visitors can indulge in a variety of delectable dishes, sip on regional wines, and enjoy live music and entertainment. With a commitment to sustainability, the festival emphasizes the use of fresh, locally sourced ingredients, providing a true taste of Devonport's gastronomic delights.

As the summer season progresses, the city transforms into a jazz enthusiast's paradise during the Devonport Jazz Festival, typically held in July. This musical extravaganza attracts jazz aficionados and performers from around the country, turning Devonport into a hub of rhythmic energy. The festival features a diverse lineup of performances, from intimate jazz club settings to open-air concerts along the waterfront. Jazz enthusiasts can immerse themselves in the soulful tunes that echo through the city, fostering an appreciation for this timeless genre.

Devonport's commitment to fostering a vibrant arts community is further evident in the annual Devonport Eisteddfod. This multi-disciplinary competition, held in August, provides a platform for local talents to showcase their skills in music, dance, drama, and the visual arts. Participants of all ages come together to compete and celebrate the arts, contributing to the city's cultural diversity. The Devonport Eisteddfod not only nurtures emerging talents but also encourages a sense of camaraderie among the participants and their supporters.

As spring blooms, the city hosts the Bloomin' Tulips Festival, a floral extravaganza that takes place in October. Embracing the beauty of the season, the festival showcases vibrant tulip displays, horticultural exhibitions, and garden tours. Visitors can wander through the tulip fields, marveling at the array of colors and fragrances that blanket the landscape. The festival's festive atmosphere extends beyond the flowers, with live music, food stalls, and family-friendly activities adding to the allure of this blooming celebration.

Devonport's maritime history takes center stage in November during the Devonport Maritime Festival. This event pays homage to the city's seafaring heritage, featuring maritime displays, boat races, and activities that highlight the importance of the sea to Devonport's identity. The waterfront comes alive with the sights and sounds of nautical festivities, providing a unique opportunity for both locals and visitors to connect with the maritime traditions that have shaped the city.

Christmas in Devonport is a magical affair, marked by the annual Devonport Christmas Parade. Usually held in early December, this festive procession winds its way through the streets of the city, adorned with twinkling lights and adorned floats. Families gather to witness the spectacle, which includes Santa's grand entrance, live music, and a joyful atmosphere that heralds the holiday season. The parade not only spreads cheer but also brings the community together in the spirit of celebration.

In addition to these major events, Devonport hosts a variety of smaller gatherings, markets, and cultural activities throughout the year. From art exhibitions and community markets to sporting events and educational workshops, there's always something happening in Devonport to cater to diverse interests.

Devonport's festivals and events form an integral part of the city's identity, bringing together residents and visitors alike to celebrate the richness of its culture, art, and community spirit.

Whether indulging in culinary delights at the Food and Wine Festival, grooving to jazz rhythms during the Jazz Festival, or marveling at blooming tulips in spring, each event contributes to the vibrant tapestry that makes Devonport a must-visit destination throughout the year. So, whether you're a local looking to immerse yourself in the city's festivities or a traveler seeking a unique cultural experience, Devonport's calendar of events offers something for everyone, ensuring an unforgettable journey of celebration and joy.

Water Activities

Devonport, the charming coastal city on the north-western shores of Tasmania, is not only a gateway to the island state but also a haven for water enthusiasts seeking a myriad of aquatic adventures. From serene river cruises to adrenaline-pumping water sports, Devonport offers a diverse range of water activities that cater to all levels of enthusiasts, ensuring an unforgettable experience against the backdrop of the city's picturesque coastal landscape.

One of the quintessential water activities in Devonport is exploring the Mersey River. The river, which meanders through the heart of the city, provides the perfect setting for a leisurely paddle or a scenic boat tour. Kayaking and canoeing are popular choices for those seeking a more hands-on and intimate connection with the water. Local operators, such as Mersey Bluff Caravan Park and Tasmanian Canoe Adventures, offer equipment rental and guided tours, allowing visitors to navigate the gentle currents while taking in the beauty of Devonport from a unique perspective.

For a more relaxed water experience, embark on a river cruise. Companies like Spirit of the Sea Cruises provide informative and enjoyable tours along the Mersey River. These cruises often include commentary on the region's history, wildlife, and points of interest, making it an ideal way to soak in the sights while sitting back and enjoying the journey. The Mersey River's scenic beauty, with its lush riverbanks and panoramic views, ensures that every cruise is a serene and rejuvenating experience.

Devonport's coastal location also makes it a prime spot for fishing enthusiasts. The city's fishing charter operators, such as Reel Time Fishing Charters, offer guided trips that cater to both novices and seasoned anglers. Whether casting a line for the thrill of the catch or simply enjoying the tranquility of the open waters, these fishing excursions provide a unique opportunity to connect with Tasmania's rich marine ecosystem.

Adventurous spirits can indulge in the excitement of jet boating on the Mersey River. Jet boat operators, like Wild Mersey, offer thrilling rides that combine high-speed maneuvers with scenic exploration. With the wind in your hair and the adrenaline pumping, jet boating adds an exhilarating dimension to the water activities available in Devonport.

Devonport's coastal charm extends to its pristine beaches, making it an ideal destination for water sports enthusiasts. Coasters Beach, East Devonport Beach, and Back Beach are popular spots for swimming, surfing, and kiteboarding. Local surf schools provide lessons for those new to the waves, ensuring a safe and enjoyable experience for all skill levels. The beaches also offer a tranquil setting for beachcombing, picnicking, or simply basking in the sun with the sound of waves as your soundtrack.

For those who prefer to stay dry but still want to appreciate the marine life, a visit to the Bass Strait Maritime Centre is a must. Located on Kelly Street, the center not only provides a fascinating insight into Tasmania's maritime history but also features interactive exhibits, including a virtual underwater experience, allowing visitors to explore the depths of the sea without getting wet.

Devonport's commitment to water-based recreation is not limited to daytime activities. The city's waterfront comes alive during the evening with the mystical glow of twilight cruises. These sunset excursions, often offered by various tour operators, provide a romantic and enchanting way to witness the changing colors of the sky over the Mersey River while enjoying a leisurely cruise.

Devonport's abundance of water activities caters to a diverse range of interests and skill levels. Whether you're seeking the thrill of adventure, a peaceful paddle along the river, or the excitement of reeling in a catch, Devonport's water offerings are as varied as the tides that lap its shores. With its stunning coastal vistas and a wealth of aquatic experiences, Devonport stands as a beacon for water enthusiasts eager to make a splash in Tasmania's aquatic wonderland.

Made in the USA
Las Vegas, NV
09 December 2023

82461020R00056